SHARED CARE OR DIVIDED LIVES?

What's best for children when parents separate

Second Edition

Dr Phil Watts

Copyright

This book is subject to copyright. Apart from that permitted under the *Copyright Act 1968* (Commonwealth), no portion can be reproduced or copied in any form, or by any means, without prior written permission from the author.

Second Edition

Ogilvie Publishing
PO Box 393
South Perth, 6951
Western Australia

 A catalogue record for this book is available from the National Library of Australia

Editing and indexing by Pickawoowoo
Typesetting and printing by

(C) P Watts, 2024

ISBN 978-0-9924121-4-2 (Paperback)

Dedication

This book is dedicated to my children, Jarom and Lorien, who successfully made it to adulthood with both their parents as an intact family. They never experienced the trauma of parental separation but helped me understand what it takes to raise responsible children.

Secondly, I dedicate this book to my eternal partner Bethwyn who is my co-parent in this parenting journey. An amazing mother and dedicated partner, I could not have asked for better.

Finally, this book is also dedicated to all the children who were not so lucky and are subject to the difficulties associated with parental break-up.

Acknowledgements

When writing the first edition I realised there is a book inside everyone and the trouble is getting it out. Even as an author of half a dozen books, I still recognise that book writing needs a support team.

Family law is a complex area to work in and I continue to be amazed at the resilience of children despite what their parents are doing to their world. I have met thousands of little teachers, the children of separating parents in the Family Court, sharing their meanings and messages with me. Meeting with these little souls, who are dealing with terribly big issues, has been a special learning experience. I have a profound respect for both their resilience and survival. I hope this book may make the journey a little easier for at least a few of them.

A special thanks goes to those in the legal profession. I have learnt about law and its many processes by my association with various independent children's lawyers, barristers, magistrates and judges. The world of family law is constantly criticised by disgruntled families who at times allege bias and complain about mistreatment. My legal colleagues are dedicated to their work and continue despite the attacks, and I have great respect for their diligence within their sphere of operations.

I have many colleagues in the profession of psychology who have helped me in my career and professional understanding. I would include a special mention of colleagues within the field of child custody evaluation, both nationally and internationally. I am careful about naming anyone for fear of leaving someone out. However, I would especially mention Phil Stahl, Robert Simon, Jenni Neoh, Lorraine Sheridan and Simon Kennedy for all they have done to encourage me within the field.

Also, a special acknowledgment of the magistrates and judges of the family courts, who through their judgments have given me knowledge about how psychological evidence is perceived in court. I have been impressed by their willingness to consider psychological information to assist them in making hard legal decisions. I realise I am a piece of evidence which can be of assistance to them when they make their challenging decisions.

A special thanks to my loving wife Bethwyn for her belief in me, her critical thinking and the practical support which allows me to write. My two delightful children, Jarom and Lorien, who not only inspire me to be a better person but show me how blessed children can be when life is stable. I wish all children could have the same opportunities they have had for a near normal life, at least as normal as a psychologist father can provide!

CONTENTS

DEDICATION	III
ACKNOWLEDGEMENTS	V
PREFACE	1
INTRODUCTION	7
CHAPTER 1 – FAMILY BREAK-UP AS A PROCESS	23
History of Divorce	23
Implications of Shared Care	27
The Separating Parents	33
Emotions of Separation	38
Money Matters	43
Trust and Perception	46
CHAPTER 2 – DEVELOPMENTAL ISSUES FOR CHILDREN	51
Child Development, Attachment and Survival	51
The Task of Growing Up	59
Decision Making Capacity in Children	65
Coping Options	70
Managing Change	79
CHAPTER 3 – PARENTAL FACTORS	83
Parental Behaviours	93
My Time with the Children	97
Overburdening the Child	100
Loyalty Demands	104
Show of Emotions	107
The Rights of the Child	109
Parental Communication	112
Parents Doing Really Badly	117
Family Violence	124
Parenting Styles	133
The United Front	142
Neuro-atypical, ADHD and Separation	145
Some Practical Parenting Points	151

CHAPTER 4 – REACHING AGREEMENT	159
Judges	170
Lawyers	172
Children and Court	174
A Voice but Not a Choice	178
Mediation and Friendship	183
Assertiveness and Other Myths	189
Strategy and Boundaries	193
CHAPTER 5 – SHARED CARE AND OTHER OPTIONS	199
Children's Factors in Parenting Arrangements	208
Visitation for other children	215
Nesting	227
Children Who Refuse Contact	230
The Case for No Contact or Change of Residence	238
Substance Abuse and Addiction	242
Separating Siblings	246
CHAPTER 6 – FINAL WORDS	251
Strive to Thrive	251
Conclusion	256
INDEX	263
ABOUT THE AUTHOR	267

Preface

Preface to Second Edition

I wrote the first edition in 2006 when family law in Australia was reformed by legislation which made equal care the primary starting point for the courts to consider. My reaction at the time was that children were not able to be cookie cut into a single shape but needed to be considered in all their varieties. In other words, arrangements needed to suit the children, not the children suit the arrangement. It has only taken 18 years but the law in Australia reformed again in 2024 where the first priority is safety and the second priority is what is best for the child without prescribing equal shared care as a starting point. Seems like the legislation has finally caught up with me!

Since writing the first book, I am now more seasoned. I have around 35 years in family law and have been the Single

Expert witness in over 2200 cases. I have trained a number of new practitioners into the profession. In doing so I am constantly reflecting on the recommendations I am making and the research upon which they are built. I am pleased to say I am not writing the second edition due to drastic change of recommendations. Rather I am better able to nuance what may be workable.

In addition, I have written this edition to extend the range of the book. The idea of my first edition was to give those who were not in court, or on the edge of court, advice on how to do it well for the kids. In this edition, I have added some chapters on dealing with harder cases. I want to address the issues of parents behaving badly and how that impacts children. There is about 25 per cent more content to draw ideas from.

My first edition has sold around ten thousand copies. I am hoping this new edition will be even more popular and practical than the edition which had gone before.

Preface to First Edition (2007)

If the title *Shared Care or Divided Lives* appealed to you, then there are at least two possible reasons why you have picked up this book. The first reason is that you are a parent or family member whose life has been touched by the terrible tragedy of a family break-up. As rates of divorce continue to rise in Australia and relationships become more temporary and disposable, more and more children are being affected. This book is written specifically for you, to help you understand in general terms some of the psychological issues which affect children in these circumstances. There is not a complete answer but this book offers some ideas about how children are affected and what living arrangements are best for them. Most importantly, this book is packed with advice on how not to compound the damage caused by separation by adding other issues to the children through your actions.

The second reason for reading this book relates to professionals who are in dire need of information about what is best for children in the aftermath of the demise of a relationship. As such you may well be a professional person associated with the Family Court arena, be it psychologist, lawyer, barrister or judge; or you may be a counsellor or mediator assisting the couple negotiate the best interests of the child. This book is designed to also assist your understanding of the dynamics children experience during the difficulties associated with family break-up. I have not written this book as a technical reference but as a way of outlining general principles, in lay terms, which hopefully will assist you in achieving the best interests of the children.

While this book is written in the context of major political and social changes in the area of family law, the purpose of this book is not part of a political agenda. If anything, it is for a psychological agenda. That agenda is to assist children by informing key decision makers about some of the implications of the choices they may make. As either parent or professional you have a tremendous responsibility for the little lives which are being affected by these decisions. I offer the sobering warning that the decisions you are making today may have permanent ramifications for the emotional health, psychological development and personality formation of the child. In the case of young children, these changes may be irreversible and the window of opportunity in actioning the best strategy may be limited.

As a forensic psychologist, I have seen first-hand the tremendous impact that divorce and parental separation has upon children. I have been appointed as an independent court expert (called "Single Expert" in the Family Court) in over 500 complex Family Court cases and as a result I have interviewed or assessed about 1000 children in the most difficult divorces possible. I have provided treatment to numerous children and their families. Therefore, I have had the opportunity to hear their views, witness first-hand the causes of their problems, and observe the impact of parental actions.

In conducting these assessments, I have seen parents psychologically tear their children to pieces in the name of winning. I have also seen many parents trying to buffer the children from the significant forces of an oppositional partner. The latter deserve the greatest of credit for their valiant attempts at trying to shelter the tender hearts of little children from intense pressure.

Children are not neutral players in the conflict but active participants. Consider the case of two children fighting. A parent will get between them and tell them to, "Stop that you two." When parents fight, children will bring forward all of their learning to the situation they find themselves. They will tell their parents to "stop that you two" and then feel disillusioned by the double standards. More profoundly, children are biologically designed to survive. The essential elements of life are not just food and water, but also love. In an orphanage, survival rates double by staff stroking infants for just five minutes a day! A child caught up in a conflict will do whatever they can to ensure the love supply continues. This may be achieved by aligning with one carer against another, or by saying what they think each parent needs to hear. An understanding of these issues is critical for assisting children to cope.

The most powerful message I hope this book can bring is the awareness that it is the behaviour of the parents, assisted by both the lay and professional advice of those around them, which is going to have the largest single impact on how children cope in this circumstance. I work on the premise all children are affected by the separation of parents; the issue is whether it is a large or small impact. The power is in your hands and I hope the information contained in this book becomes a tool which helps to minimise the damage during this dark period of a child's life.

Key points

- The factors which have the greatest impact upon children in a parental separation are the emotions, reactions and behaviours of each parent. The better a parent understands this, the more they can help their children.

- There is no such thing as neutral behaviour. Everything a parent does impacts upon the children. Make every action count for the greater good of the child.

- All children are affected by parental separation. The choice a parent has is whether to shield them from the issues, or damage them.

Introduction

I asked each of six children, who varied in age from 2 to 10 years, what they called their father. The answer was the same from all of them. They called him 'thing'. When I asked them to explain what they meant they said, *"He is not a dad, he is not a father, he is a thing."* On further explanation, the three oldest children said that on a Friday night they stayed up later than normal with their mother. They ate pizza, watched TV and celebrated no 'thing' in the house. They called Friday night "no-thing club".

Had the father been a member of an outlaw motorcycle gang, a violent criminal or mentally deranged, there might have been some justification in the attitudes of the children (not that such attitudes will help the children's psychological development). While he most certainly had some issues, the father in this case did not have that type of pathology. A complicated set of factors led this mother to act in such a manner, issues which professional confidentiality prevents me from expressing. Even without knowing the details, one cannot help but wonder about the horrendous impact that such action will have on her children's long-term psychological wellbeing. The clear short-term gain was that none of the children wanted to have anything to do with their father. It was impossible to re-establish a relationship between the children and their father, as he had not been able to see them for about 12 months. The prospects of future contact were negligible with such intense views. The mother won the short-term battle, but the cost will be a life-time of problems for the children.

Although it is some 25 years since seeing this case, I still think about it from time to time and wonder how these children have adjusted to life, particularly as they reached adulthood. I wonder about the impact on their ability to form relationships, how they are going to deal with conflict when problems arise, and the impact upon them from the loss of a male role model. The list of possible psychological impacts goes on. I would not expect them to remain unscathed by the process and the damage is unlikely to be reversed by a stepfather. A father cannot be replaced by an exchange model. The international research supports my views that the actions can be quite psychologically damaging.

One way of understanding the impact is to consider that children are biologically half of each parent. When you consider how children are discussed within families you hear descriptions like you have "your mother's eyes" or "your father's cute little dimple". If one parent is being rejected you begin to see how half of the child's self is rejected. However, family descriptions of traits also go to emotions or behavioural characteristics such as "you get anxious just like granny Jones", "you have your father's anger", or "you carry on like your mother". Where one parent rejects the other parent in the presence of the child, half of that child's identity is being rejected. Even if the alienating mother or father remarries, the best the child can hope for is a reasonable role model. They will never find the missing half of their identity in the new man or woman. Each child in the case above is half the mother and half a thing!

At the time when I assessed this family I felt somewhat powerless in terms of finding solutions to help the children re-establish a relationship with their father. As a forensic psychologist I began to study in depth the behaviour of parents during separation situations so as to develop strategies for the future to overcome the blatant influence associated with these sorts of cases. Sadly, the reality is that courts can order time and place but cannot order children or parents to change their attitudes. Legal solutions to bad parenting are limited.

The treatment is exceptionally difficult in the case of rejecting parents. After a year or so of separation from one parent, and having established such strong attitudes, will the children be better off being removed from the isolating parent so they can see the other parent, or should that other parent miss out on seeing their children? If the option is to remove the children and place them with the other parent, do you put them into foster care if they then refuse to live with him or her? Foster care is not a neutral option as the children are removed from loving familiar people to go to caring strangers. Maybe it is possible to try to set up some type of contact with children, but what if they refuse to go on visits or, if they do go, they do not want to stay? Alternatively, if the children stay with an isolating parent, the impact upon the children will be profound.

Sadly, 25 years later, although I am somewhat wiser in terms of the dynamics, I am still at a loss to make recommendations that will guarantee a change in the course of such cases once the pattern has become ingrained. There is no formula that can fix it, and as indicated above, the court is limited in what it can do. There are no neutral courses of action. I have learnt about a lot of things which do not work, and some things which may work some of the time.

The only consistent answer I can find at this stage lies not in what is done with the children but in changing the attitude of the parents. It is only through helping parents realise their choices, and setting up situations where they can exercise those choices in a more positive fashion, that the damage will be minimised. My hope is that early intervention through professional education and books like this will prevent some cases reaching such destructive levels.

The example I have used was one of the worst cases in which I have had first-hand experience. I deliberately used this significant case to make a point. However, it is critical to note that all actions lie on a continuum from supporting to undermining the alternate parent. The person may be an ex-partner but they are never a child's ex-parent. Children are permanently connected to their biological heritage and the full impact of this comes as their identity develops during their teens onwards.

The micro world of an individual family break-up also must be considered against the macro environment of the wider community. Courts are not about fair, right or justice, they are about applying rules to problems. The solutions a court can apply will only come from what the rules say. Australia, like most other Western countries, is undergoing changes to try to make the rules work for children. Australia had legislation, the *Family Law Amendment (Shared Parental Responsibility) Act* 2006 (Commonwealth), which proposed a starting point for equal shared care – the presumption both parents have an equal involvement in the children's lives, and both parents have a meaningful involvement. That legislation stipulates that equal shared care must be considered.

The reality is that while some children in Australia have equal shared care and like it, the problem is that sharing care requires parents to work together to make it effective. Once families are in court the ability to work together is reduced or non-existent. In 2024, the legislation removed the requirement to have equal time considered as the starting point but for the court to consider what is best for the child. It is an important distinction which we will revisit though this book. What is best for the children is not always what is best for the parents.

After nearly 20 years of the shared care legislation the change has not been remarkable. Sadly about 49 per cent of children are not seeing enough of the other parent to have any overnight time. This figure of about half of children not having any substantive time with the other parent has not changed in decades, while a staggering 26 per cent never see the other parent. While society has seen a profound shift in the social expectations in the roles of parents (e.g. the concept of the traditional wife at home caring for children and the father working to provide for the family has faded dramatically), the sharing of the care of children has seen some change but it is not remarkable.

A 2003 Australian Bureau of Statistics study found that of the 1.3 million children aged birth to 17 years old, who were in families where a natural parent lived elsewhere, only a third were seeing the other parent more often than once per fortnight. When it comes to sleeping over, the proportion of children staying for 30 per cent or more nights (equivalent to an average of two nights per week) with the other natural parent was a tiny 6 per cent. This was up from 3 per cent in 1997. The statistics show that in 2021 the percentage in Australia was around 11.6 per cent – that includes both shared and equal time. Therefore, both prior to the legislation and after, there has been an increase in the percentage of children staying for meaningful time in the household of both parents, but it is still only a small percentage of all the children in separated families.

Major social changes will need to continue if these percentages are to increase. Take a simple example; if two parents are to share equally in the day-to-day care of the children, the single parent, currently at home, will be required to work in order to survive financially, while the other parent, currently working, will have to reduce their working hours to attend to the children. In both cases, the way in which society structures work will need to change. It is outside of my writing here to advise on issues of economic inequality and gender roles, but these are central to change. Children need to be valued more than work alone, and both parents need to be able to afford the children.

This shared care opens up interesting options, both good and bad, for families. The good is most evident in the opportunity for children, after their parents have separated, to have meaningful relationships with both parents but especially their fathers. I say "fathers" due to statistics – not because of gender bias. The research continues to find that children were more likely to live with their mother than their father after parents separated. The research shows that in more than 80 per cent of cases it was the father who was the natural parent living elsewhere. In some parts of the world the proportion of children living with their fathers has increased markedly, but this has not been the case in Australia over the last 30 years. Interestingly, men as single fathers are far more likely to look after older children. About 56 per cent of the children in the primary care of their fathers were in their teens, while only about 9 per cent were under four years.

In the past, most children in parental separations had insufficient time with their fathers. The changed society will give fathers a much better opportunity. The statistics suggest fathers were more likely to care for the children when they were more independent and perhaps more difficult to care for. Therefore, fathering in Australia will have to undergo a major renaissance to effectively make the necessary changes. While there have always been some exceptional fathers taking on the full-time care of children, including small children, the statistics indicate the vast majority of fathers must change the way they do things.

A positive impact reflected in the research literature is that after a couple separations, fathers spend more one-on-one time with the children compared to pre-separation. In a relationship the parents and children go out as a family. After separation, the father is doing it on his own to a greater degree. The children get more direct parenting time from their father if the father is involved after separation, notwithstanding the shocking numbers earlier about children who do not see the other parent.

Similarly, the role of women will need to undergo major change. Even though women have been campaigning for decades for equal opportunity in the workplace, for many women there is a very deep psychological significance in being a mother and for their identity to be defined by this role. To share parenting time, women will be required to give up time with their children and consequently change how they view their role. This is a threatening prospect for many women. Like men in the 1960s and 1970s who had their work identity changed by laws giving women more rights, women will now have to deal with changes they may not necessarily want in their lives. I am seeing this change being more widely accepted but it still has a long way to go for both men and women.

From the perspective of the child, the implications of shared care are also profound. In a case where I was asked to do an assessment of two high-functioning parents disagreeing over the final workings of a shared-care arrangement, the mother said to me that what she wanted was a shared-care arrangement, but what the father was proposing in her terms was a *"divided life"*. The back story to this case was she was a nurse who could work weekends and earn penalty rates. The father was an engineer working weekday hours. It suited her to have the child during the week, and him to have the child on the weekend. The child was a little person, still under three years old. She started to become upset when mum left (normal attachment stage as you will read later in the book). The father applied what I call an engineering solution. If the child gets upset when mum leaves, then if she does not come over, she will not leave and the child will not become upset. He banned the mother from seeing the child during "his time" (I dedicate a whole section to this toxic term later in the book). In the mother's mind, shared care consisted of two parents having an active involvement in the child's life, doing similar things through overlapping contact.

What her partner was proposing were two relatively separate periods with no overlapping involvement. For her it was like the father was dividing the life of the child rather than sharing the care of the child.

Upon reflection, it was evident her feelings summed up the attitude of many parents, particularly women, where they would ideally love to be able to share the care of the children; however, they are being forced into arrangements where this will not be possible because of legally binding structures effectively dividing the child's time into "his" and "her" time. Having worked in the Family Court system for a number of years it is evident to me that this is going to be an ongoing problem. There are people who cannot agree on parenting factors, and there are certainly parents who lack the capacity to be able to structure a shared arrangement. If the parents cannot share the care, the implications are the children in these arrangements will have a divided life.

The fundamental issue is to assist key decision-makers to understand what children need after their parents separate so the children can get the best life possible, not a divided life. Shared care is not about splitting time into two parcels. It is about a child having a seamless transition between two slightly different environments. The law can only stipulate how time is to be divided. Parents have to make that time shared time, often under difficult circumstances (i.e. trying to work in the best interests of their children while dealing with someone they may not like). It is ironic that a couple breaks up because they are no longer compatible with each other, or have difficulties relating to each other, and yet society says they must work together in the interests of the children. A lawyer once said to me there is no such thing as retrospective contraception, you cannot "un-have" the child with that parent!

To help explain the needs of children, I have divided this book into five main sections. The first section is an overview of how parents cope during separation, as well as touching on some of the more concerning issues occurring between parents, such as family violence. It is important to understand the emotional processes associated with separation – whether married or de facto, heterosexual or LGBQTI – are going to impact the parents' ability to cope, and it is one of the most important factors affecting the way in which children adapt. One of my primary arguments in this book is that the way in which parents act in the separation process will have the biggest emotional impact upon the children's emotional adjustment. The process of separation affects parents profoundly, particularly their ability to be rational in their decision-making in the early part of the separation process. Consequently, the first chapter of the book addresses the separation process to help put the actions of parents into context.

Not only do the parents have a huge impact on how children cope, the personality and nature of the children themselves is a critical variable. There are some children who are robust and cope with change readily, and there are other children who tend to be anxious about change and find difficulty adjusting. As a father of twins I see this in my own children. Just dealing with simple situations such as going to a party at three years of age, my little girl readily went forward and wanted to mix, whereas my son would hold back until he was more certain of what was happening. At 15 years old it was the reverse, with my daughter having anxiety and my son being more inclined to socialise with people he did not know. If I had to translate their behaviour to work out a schedule for overnight access, my daughter would cope with a much wider range of variations than would my son at three but would be different at 15. The fact the two of them were close means keeping them together would have improved the chances of my son going on overnight visits at three years of age, but they lost some of that closeness in their teen years and may have done better with separate arrangements at that point of their lives. Consequently, developmental factors, coupled with children's personalities, are very important considerations in the sharing mix. I discuss these factors in Chapter Two.

The issues touched on in the example of the father being called 'thing' need to be understood before examining the impact of different visiting arrangements upon children. There are a number of behaviours parents can engage in that are extremely destructive to the psychological wellbeing of children. This book does not aim to catalogue all those negative behaviours. Rather, I will describe in Chapter Three some of the situations that significantly impact the dynamics.

On the reverse side, there are a number of behaviours which parents can engage in which maximise the chances of the child coping in a separation situation. I will describe some of these behaviours to provide you with an opportunity for positive change. Therefore, Chapter Three also examines positive parental behaviour which helps to facilitate adjustment of children in separation and conflict situations. I would like you to take note of these factors in particular because once you separate you can only control what is on your side of the bridge. Too many times I see fingers pointing at what the ex-partner may have done or may be doing but the person can have no control over any of this. You can only control what you do, and you have to be the bigger person.

To reach agreement, there are only a handful of options in the conflict of a family breakdown. The first of these is parents working it out themselves. Notably about 65 per cent of parents sort out their own arrangements and only need to use the court to ratify their arrangements. It may not be fun but at least it was your decision. The second option is that the parents work the arrangements out with the assistance of a third person such as a mediator. Mediation is enough to push some people over the line. However, there are some people who have to be arbitrated as they will not agree. They need to have a legal solution imposed by an independent arbitrator such as a judge. The amount of control which a parent has over the outcome diminishes as the solutions are imposed by others. Therefore, the best outcome for children will come from solutions parents agree with, or even if they do not fully agree, at least have input into making. Chapter Four considers some of the factors involved in reaching a favourable agreement.

Chapter Five is devoted to the impact of differing arrangements for scheduling visits. Under the law in Australia, this is called "time with" each parent. If you have picked up this book hoping to find a definitive arrangement, I am sorry to disappoint you, but the research literature has not pointed out a single best arrangement. There are different arrangements possible, and within those arrangements the impacts will vary depending on the age of the children, the way the parents relate, assorted personality variables and a host of other factors. I do not have a magic formula or even any simple solutions. In fact, at separation, children will only ever get less time with their parents than they did before a separation, unless one or both parents cease work.

Perhaps the easiest way to explain the overall impact of parental separation is as follows. When two parents live together, a child in that arrangement is in a position of being able to have 200 per cent care – 100 per cent from each parent. It is rare that parents are available 24 hours a day, seven days a week as life factors such as work, study, school, recreation, house-keeping and other activities will impinge on parental availability. Occasionally, families may travel around the country together, or in rare situations such as the lock-down during the pandemic, children may get a full 200 per cent. The maximum possible care in a separated relationship is not half of that, but effectively a quarter. In an equally shared arrangement, each parent is only able to have the child 50 per cent of the time, and of that time the parents are still struggling with their normal work, study, house-keeping and recreational activities, compounded by the fact they are having to do it all alone. The only way to change these percentages is to increase the overlapping time, such as both attending the sports activity on Saturday (if appropriate).

There may be a small spin-off of positive factors such as an uninvolved father prior to separation, who was working long hours and only spending time with the children and the mother, may actually have an increase in quality time post-separation because he values the time he now has with the children, and for the first time is now spending long periods with them on his own. However, the net effect of the percentage dropping from 200 per cent to 50 per cent is that children are going to miss out badly, irrespective of whatever arrangement is put in place.

The fifth chapter of this book offers an examination of different living arrangements. While the professionals who work with the court need formal structured arrangements, there needs to be consideration of how the arrangements will impact all children, regardless of circumstance. Dealing with the Family Court will be one of the most stressful events a parent may ever experience in their life. Fortunately, the vast majority of cases are solved without requiring Family Court intervention, and a fair proportion of those which do become active cases in the Family Court settle rather than follow through to a trial. For anyone involved in this process I offer my deepest sympathy because of the highly stressful nature of this experience.

In considering the content of this book, I should warn the reader that the psychological research is not yet in on many aspects of the questions we need answered. Therefore, when a country changes their legislation, they engage the country in a vast social experiment, with the final outcome unlikely to be known for a generation. Many social scientists in the family research area are currently examining the issues I raise here, and therefore new information will come to light in coming years. In providing this second edition, I was pleasantly surprised at how few of the fundamental psychological building blocks for the best interests of children leading to good outcomes from separation, had been changed by the research. The core recommendations of *Shared Care or Divided Lives* remains consistent.

Key points

- Separation means that children go from having a possible 200 per cent of parental involvement (100 per cent from each parent), to a maximum of 50 per cent (half-time with each individual parent). All children lose out with separation.

- Relatively few children (less than 11.6 per cent of separated families) are currently in any form of shared care, and less than 6 per cent are in equal care. There will need to be significant social changes to make shared care work at a practical level.

- The positive benefit of the recent shared care legislation in Australia is that it opens up new possibilities for children to have two parents actively involved in their lives. Children are going to be better off if they can develop meaningful relationships with both parents, especially if they can get better relationships with their fathers, given that most already have a relationship with their mothers.

- There are likely to be profound implications for children from shared care, and parents need to consider what is best for children, not what is fair for parents.

- Children are biologically and psychologically half of each parent. Reject the other parent and half of the child is being rejected. Please keep the children whole, despite the feelings involved.

1
Family Break-Up As A Process

History of Divorce

Family relationships have undergone an extraordinary revolution within Australia, and the rest of the Western world, during the past 150 years. Marriage has changed from a sacred institution to be preserved at almost any cost, to something that can be dissolved on a no-fault basis when it has irretrievably broken down. While this section documents the situation in Australia, it mirrors similar processes throughout the Western world. Many of these changes happened universally, the main issue is which country leads the changes and who was slow to follow.

Australia, when colonised, inherited its divorce laws from England. Under those laws, divorces were rare. It could only be granted on the grounds of adultery, and the prevailing double standard considered that adultery by a woman constituted a reason for marriage break-up, while a wife was not seen to be seriously prejudiced if her husband engaged in a single act of adultery. This was hardly surprising given divorce laws were primarily about property, and women and children were defined as property by the law. It was the case under common law that a mother's right to the custody of her children was completely subordinate to that of the child's father, and that the child's father could claim possession of the child, even taking a suckling child from the mother's breast. This happened irrespective of how wicked the man may have been. Children were in effect property belonging to the man. The single-parent home existed in small numbers, but under the law a child born out of wedlock was classified as a "bastard" and support was therefore negligible.

Over the course of the 1900s the shoe was shifted to the other foot. Children went to the mothers and fathers now had difficulty seeing the children. Mothers had to be shown to be unfit to lose custody of the children. This change first started in the 1850s, when drunkenness of men and the desertion of their wives was seen as a problem in Australia, so the law of divorce was extended to include abandonment as grounds for divorce and to provide for the maintenance of these women. Australia also found the inherited British attitudes to be extreme, and the rights of women were hotly debated. Over the next hundred years change was relatively slow but increasingly recognised the plight of deserted wives, the need for financial support, and the custody and interests of the children. For example, in 1928, legislation was passed in regard to guardianship of children (giving custody to the woman), and the welfare of children was of paramount concern – a significant change for women and children. These changes reflected the beginnings of the "tender years" presumption – children during their early years needed to be cared for by their mothers, probably due to the prevailing attitudes that raising children was women's work.

In 1975, the Whitlam government introduced legislation which still underpins the legislation today. Whitlam's government introduced no-fault divorce, with the single requirement that couples live apart for a year. Women had also been actively campaigning for equal rights in the workplace, and to have a role greater than that of homemaker. With marriages ending more easily, divorce rates steadily climbed. Various social changes have seen the importance of marriage fade and de facto relationships increasingly being recognised by the law. As it stands currently, approximately 72 per cent of children aged from newborn to 17 years of age in Australia live in intact families. The remainder are in single-parent families or blended relationships.

In 2006, the law introduced the concept of equal time as a starting precept. It had to be considered if it was practical, and whether it was in the best interests of the children. The lead-up to these changes had already seen a shift towards equal time, but this law formalised the era we are now in. The deciding factors for children after separation are no longer property rights of fathers, nor the tender years presumption leading to care by mothers, but what is best for children. It is now about the child's "best interests". The 2024 legislation is making it even clearer that the safety and best interests of the children should be the priority of the court.

Therefore, in the space of a single generation, we have seen a rapid escalation of divorce rates, and large numbers of children now being raised in various combinations of families which are intact, separated and re-partnered and, in some cases, families with several new partners resulting in a very complex mix of parentage for the children. What was once "living in sin" is now seen as a sensible "try before you buy". Society has become increasingly focused on the individual and, as a result, if an individual is unhappy in a relationship, the relationship is terminated, and the parties move on. This has been called "serial monogamy". People have one partner at a time, but when they get sick of one partner, they find another. This is the age of disposable relationships. Parents are choosing to separate because they are unhappy, have some incompatibilities, have 'fallen out' of love, or for a range of other reasons. I would also add that within a period of a few decades, same sex marriage and the legal status of de facto relationships have been recognised by society. While taken for granted today, these are very recent changes. Even the word divorce does not apply to many situations as many couples are having children without marriage, something rare in the past but normal by today's expectations. Separation, rather than divorce, is a more appropriate term to cover parents who break up whether married or not.

Key points

- The nature of divorce in Australia has changed from finding fault to that of no blame, making it easier than ever to separate. Similarly, relationships can now exist without marriage. Parents owe it to their children to seriously attempt to fix their relationship prior to commencing the separation process.

- The legal position of children in separation has changed from children being the property of the father, to the placement of a child of tender years with the mother, to the best interests of child, to equal care, and now back to the best interests of the child.

Implications of Shared Care

While it is the right of the parents to form a new relationship, it is the parents who have the choice and control. It is the children who do not have a choice. Therefore, the best interests of children are not necessarily the same as the best interests of the parents. It follows that although the law allows us to consider the best interests of children in the process of separating families, a child rarely sees parental separation as in their own best interest. It is a trauma inflicted upon them.

From the perspective of me being a voice for children, I would argue that two parents staying together and learning to have a functional relationship would best serve the children's interests. At risk of being too provocative, is the parents' right to be happy greater than the children's right to be happy and have a stable upbringing? It is probably too late by the time you are reading this book, but staying for the sake of the children has some merit for the children (as long as the parent or children are not unsafe). All children are impacted by the separation of parents but the better they can understand the process the more they can deal with the process using logic and understanding.

In cases where there is extreme conflict, and particularly violence, the literature is categorically clear that children will be better off away from that circumstance. Danger to a parent or child is one of the few genuine circumstances where leaving the relationship will create a better situation for the children. If you are contemplating leaving a violent relationship, please ensure you seek advice on how to do it safely as the riskiest time for violence is around separation.

In lesser levels of conflict, if the safety concerns can be adequately addressed, then serious relationship counselling or individual therapy may be able improve the situation. If you can fix it, that is likely to be a better outcome for the children. This is a complex decision to make, and it is easy to find professionals who align with your view. You want out, it is easy to find someone to tell you to get out. You want to fix it, there are professionals who can help you fix it. Ultimately, you have to know what you want to do, but you will be doing this at a time when you are probably your least capable version of yourself. People are not reading this book when life is going well for them, they are reading it during one of the most difficult times of their life!

A frequently asked question is whether it is better for parents to stay together for the sake of the children or whether it is better to separate. As stated above, if the relationship is destructive then separation is usually a better option, especially if those problems cannot be fixed. However, separation is a destructive process for children. There is a growing body of research which indicates that parents who may have fallen out of love but can cohabit (without exhibiting destructive behaviour) and not break up the home cause fewer adverse effects on the children than if the parents separate. Therefore, the parents' ability to control their feelings is going to be the critical variable in the children's long-term adjustment. In these cases, children are generally better off with their two natural parents living together. My opinion is children will do best with two happy parents, so try to fix yourselves and the relationship for the sake of the children.

Another question often asked is whether there is less impact on children where the parents separate sooner (when children are younger) than later. The evidence indicates children of all ages are affected but that impact manifests in different ways depending on age and maturity. The young child whose parents separate shows all sorts of psychological disturbances but they cannot understand what is happening. Generally, parents who stay together longer are going to produce better-adjusted children (unless the children are being subject to ongoing family violence), but short-term adjustment problems can be worse with older children. Even adult children, who have left home and started families of their own, can struggle emotionally when their parents separate. It is not a simple process.

From years of observing how children cope, and coupling that understanding to the literature, I think developmentally normal children in the age range of 7 to 12 years old probably cope the best with separation. Younger children have more emotion and less understanding. Teens have a lot of issues to deal with including identity issues. However, I am not saying pre-teens are not affected, it is just they have a window to deal with the issues in ways other ages do not. (See the chapter on how children cope for more information on this important consideration.)

With the ever-increasing rights of the individual over the communal responsibility for families, people will be less inclined to try to fix their problems before leaving the relationship. It is interesting that the legislation since 2006 in Australia has required an increase in proof of mediation prior to entering the legal system. In other words, the system is legally requiring people to try to fix their disagreement prior to court. My views go further. Children are a lifetime responsibility and giving them the best chance in life is an important consideration. In other words, parents need put aside their differences to address the long-term needs of the children.

To be clear in this book I would like to define shared care. Shared care is commonly defined in the professional literature as both parents having 30-35 per cent or more of the time – usually calculated by the number of nights not hours – with the children. It applies to children typically of school age onward. Babies, infants, and pre-primary aged children are complex and I will discuss them later. The research shows shared care can result in equal relationships with the children when older. I am not saying 29 per cent is terrible and 31 per cent is guaranteed good.

Shared care can be equal, meaning it is about 50 per cent with each parent. Or it can be unequal, being 30 per cent to nearly 50 per cent. The evidence is strong that shared care with low conflict has the greatest benefits for most children going through separation. The evidence is weak or questionable as to whether the outcomes for children get better as the time increases from shared to equal time.

Equal shared care can be seen in one of two ways. It can be seen as recognising the right of parents to have similar amounts of time with children, that is, to reflect a "fairer" position in sharing time with children equally between the two households. Alternatively, it can be seen as being in the best interests of children by letting them see both parents on an equal or more meaningful basis. The first argument should not be why we do shared care. It should not be about rights of parents. The alternative argument is the one which matters. It should be good for children.

It is important to realise that in a normal household prior to separation it is rare to have equal time with the children. Most homes have parents doing different things, all important, but with different requirements. Working to provide a nice house and pay private school fees is commendable for the family but it means the parent has limited time with the children due to work commitments. Another parent may take parenting leave and have full-time availability. Some parents play sport or have other personal activities on the weekend. It is how life is for busy households. Prior to separation there may have always been a primary carer, parents may take turns, or the duties may have been close to equal. In each case, the children will be used to different arrangements. For example, in a traditional family structure where the father ran a multimillion-dollar business and the mum had been a stay-at-home mum, the children could not comprehend equal time with their father – "Why? He has never been there for us," said the 15 year old. The sad reality was that what he said was an accurate reflection of his life. Equal care did not make sense to him.

These changes toward meaningful sharing of the lives of children reflect progress in relation to their wellbeing. Three decades ago, the standard contact arrangement for fathers was every second weekend and a week in school holidays. We now have a situation where the role of the father is considered to be on an equal footing with the mother, and that children are seen as a joint responsibility. In theory this is a positive step forward and the implications for society are immense. If we can make it work in practice, the children will benefit greatly.

If true shared care were implemented on an ongoing basis, where parents have what is defined as reasonable and meaningful time including weekend and weekday involvement, it would necessitate a restructuring of employment for both fathers and mothers to enable them to participate equally in the parenting role. If there is not a restructuring of the workforce, then the net outcome will be an increase in the number of children spending time in day care and after-school care which will significantly magnify problems already associated with having less quality time with both parents.

From the child's point of view, the idea of having a meaningful relationship with both parents is an excellent proposition. However, a concerning aspect of such an approach is that it is based on parents wanting to have an equal share of the child rather than the parents working out what is best for their child. In other words, the child may be divided.

Underpinning this is another particularly concerning aspect – financial issues. As will be discussed in more detail later, when property settlement and the sharing of children become jointly connected issues, there are significant benefits flowing to a parent having a larger share of the child's time because they will get a larger share of the money, will pay less child support and be entitled to a greater percentage of the allowances. These are factors which are not related to the children's best interests but to parental entitlements. Sadly, some of the disputes I see are really about money, and the kids are the bargaining chips. Sad but true. Once again, we can see that issues of property and money are interwoven with issues of divorce and separation.

Key points

- Shared care is defined as 30 to 35 per cent or more time with the other parent, while equal shared care is near 50 per cent of the time, usually referring to the number of nights not the number of hours.

- Shared care from a child's perspective is having the opportunity to develop a reasonable and meaningful relationship with both parents. Children need both parents.

- Equal time with each parent is fair for the parents but is not necessarily what is in the best interests of the child.

- Money and sharing the time with the child are issues which should be kept separate. Do not base decisions for a child around money and property; base the decision on what is best for the child.

The Separating Parents

When I sit in my office, as a therapist assisting people deal with emotional issues, one of the most common catalysts for seeking therapy is to deal with relationship break-up issues. This is not surprising as separation is an emotionally charged adjustment, which takes a significant period of time to come to terms with.

The typical man comes into the office and begins with the statement: *"I don't know why she left me, it wasn't that bad."* As we explore the issues, he will typically say that yes, she had mentioned there were problems, but he did not consider the problems to be that serious. The typical woman on the other hand, when seeking therapy, will say: *"I told him for years and nothing ever changed. In the end I couldn't tolerate it anymore and I've left."*

In approximately 70 per cent of relationship terminations, it is the woman who leaves. Therefore, on separation, there are fundamental differences in the positions of each parent. The parent who decides to leave (typically the woman) has usually had a large period of anticipatory grieving. They are called the initiator. By that I mean she has been dealing with the emotions for years and has reached the point of resolution. For her, separation is the new beginning, and she is keen to start her new life. She is beyond further negotiation and wants to experience life outside of the oppressive environment of the family home. The initiator has done the grieving and they are ready to go.

On the other hand, for the one who is left, typically the man, the separation is a seemingly sudden experience and grieving begins on the day of separation, rather than years before that point. They are the non-initiator. Therefore, typically the emotions are running much higher for the man than for the woman. They are in the early stages of grief, shock, bargaining and at times anger. They would do anything to get the relationship back. As emotions override the brain they may engage in illogical and inappropriate emotions. For example, when men get depressed they are more likely than women to show irritability and aggression as symptoms.

I note there are other reasons relationships break up than those initiated by the woman. Some people will say they separated because they grew apart. In such cases the difference between the initiator and non-initiator may not be great, and the emotions not as strong. On the other hand, in cases where someone has cheated on another person, then the non-initiator not only has the grief from the separation but the anger from betrayal – now the emotions of the separation are on steroids! The situation may be very hard to handle.

Anyone who has read *Men are from Mars, Women are from Venus* or any other of the gender characterising books will know that while these books speak in generalisations, they become best sellers because these generalisations are widely applicable. For the separating couple many of these generalisations become readily apparent. Men tend to bottle up their feelings, reach crisis point and then act them out. Therefore, men are likely to become increasingly irrational on separation. There is a whole system geared to keep people safe, and many men who are expressing their anger and frustration then become more angry and frustrated when restraining orders prevent them from seeing their partners and children.

A very clear message I would give to men in the separation situation is they need to quickly seek assistance for dealing with their emotions, otherwise the problems will snowball for both themselves and their families. Professional counselling is necessary because men are often caught in a paradoxical situation. Society has a belief that men are supposed to be strong. Being sad is a sign of weakness. The more distressed a man gets, the more those around him may want to punish him for being weak. On the other hand, women are seen through a filter which says that women who are upset are vulnerable.

Her distress brings an increase in support, while his distress may result in isolation and rejection. Hence the need for both parties, especially the man, to get support to assist in managing emotions. The court system is very negative towards angry men and society is making family violence provisions tighter.

The typical child who has to deal with an angry, grieving father will become increasingly distressed and disturbed. If there is a lot of anger the child may become fearful. If there is a lot of sadness the child may engage in caretaking behaviour. The "caretaker child" is the one who will comfort their father while he cries, bringing the father support. Often fathers who are in this situation express their sadness and anger concurrently and this becomes very confusing for the child. This places the child in a contradictory and conflicting position. The child will often want to assist the father and exhibit caretaking behaviours, yet at the same time feel afraid of the father. If the non-initiator is a woman, then many of the same issues apply. When the child is in the "caretaker position", what this means is the parent is no longer the adult in charge. In essence, the parent has abdicated from his or her role of being the parent, in terms of making the child feel safe in the world. Neither distress nor anger on the part of the parent is going to be beneficial to the child.

As stated earlier, it is only in 30 per cent of relationships that the man initiates the separation. There are a multitude of reasons why this is so, but these cases often involve another partner. When a woman is left for someone younger, she is left to deal with a range of complex emotions associated with that process. Because it is seemingly unexpected then there is often an overwhelming array of emotions. The anger and sense of betrayal are huge. I see cases where the woman is unable to shift past these emotions and the children suffer because of her anger at the father.

Issues associated with control also apply when one partner leaves the other partner behind. The non-initiator feels helpless and powerless because, if they wanted the relationship to work or would like to give it another go, they are unable to do so because of their partner's decision. Feelings of loss of control increase the sense of powerlessness and can often trigger anxiety or depression. While there is generally a high rate of depression associated with marital break-up, the partner who is left is increasingly more vulnerable to experiencing depression.

Key Points

- In approximately 70 per cent of relationship terminations, it is the woman who leaves.

- The parent who decides to leave has usually completed a large period of anticipatory grieving. They are called the initiator. On separation they want to start their new life.

- For the one who is left, the separation is a seemingly sudden experience and grieving begins on the day of separation, rather than years before that point. They are the non-initiator. The non-initiator often has emotions running high.

Emotions of Separation

Research has been conducted on the impact of a depressed parent on children. While difficult to summarise in simple terms, the research suggests if a parent is depressed, they lack the emotional resources to meet the needs of the children. From the child's point of view, this is very frightening because, although the parent is physically available and sometimes able to conduct the physical requirements of parenting, they are emotionally "empty" and unable to comfort, soothe and make the child feel safe. Therefore, the children, during a period of high need, have a parent who is in a state where they are least able to meet those needs. With the breakdown of the extended family over the last 30 years, often there is little external support for the family. If available, these relatives can help to compensate for the child's needs while the mother or father deals with their depression. My advice in these situations is for parents to seek early and appropriate treatment for depression if they want to assist their children to the best of their capacity.

Where depression and hopelessness are present, suicidal thoughts are usually associated. Often during a separation process, one person may have suicidal thoughts. If these are passing thoughts along the lines of, *"I don't want to keep going"*, then I would argue the person is probably quite normal, and it is an escape fantasy. However, when a party starts to develop active suicidal ideation, thinking about plans or actually acting on the plans, then professional help is needed. As a therapist, I can categorically state that separation is far less damaging to a child than losing a parent to suicide. Children do not get over a parent who kills themself. If you are feeling this way seek professional help immediately.

As an aside, there is a well-established myth that depression is caused by a chemical imbalance in the brain. There is ample research to show there *is* a chemical imbalance in the brain of a person suffering from depression. However, the issue is that it is life events and stress which can cause chemical changes. There are a multitude of factors which lead the body to having a chemical imbalance; grief and negative experiences being common precipitating factors. Likewise, psychological therapy is of great assistance in pulling someone out of a reactive depression. The chemicals in the brain will change back as people deal with issues at a psychological level.

My advice to clients with respect to the treatment of depression is as follows. If the depression is mild, meaning they feel lousy but are generally coping with day-to-day life, then psychological therapy is probably the most effective treatment. If they have moderate depression, where it is interfering with some day-to-day functions and they are feeling lousy, then psychological therapy and medication would be the advisable approach. The medication is used because it is the quickest way to put in place some stability, and psychological counselling because it can address the underlying causes. In the case of severe depression, there is a definite need for urgent psychiatric treatment, and therapy may need to be put on hold until the depression has been stabilised by medication.

If you are in court, most judicial officers understand that depression is common in their clients. The key is if you are doing something about the depression they will look at you favourably, while if left untreated and it is impacting you it may lower your outcomes in the court process.

The process associated with the breaking up of a relationship is one which takes a considerable period of time to complete. There is a need to work through the issues. Even couples who recognised they were incompatible but still like each other, and were actually glad the relationship finished, take a period of time to reach adjustment. Little things like sleeping in bed alone, having to do all the joint tasks or, as a parent, not being able to nip to the supermarket for some milk without packing up the four-year-old and the six-year-old in the car for a 10-minute trip, all have a negative impact.

There is a range of common emotions associated with grief in the early parts. Often there is shock and denial. Where couples talk about having a 'trial separation' they are often in a denial and bargaining process. I am not convinced trial separations have any value. Stay together and work it out, or separate, don't prolong the agony. As the shock wears off the common feelings are anger and depression. How quickly these are worked through is difficult to quantify because that depends on a person's life experience, past baggage and the circumstances of the break-up. For example, a couple who have separated due to mutual incompatibility will have a very different course to a couple who have broken up because of one party's infidelity.

Every couple talks about "being friends". Psychologically it is a relatively easy process to go from an acquaintance to a friend to a lover. The deepening of a relationship by the sharing of experiences follows a very natural course. However, it is quite an unnatural course to then go from being a lover, where one is sharing all aspects of their mind and body, to go back to being social acquaintances. The goal of "let's be friends" is certainly a lofty but appropriate ideal to achieve. My general advice is it is unlikely to be achieved in the first two years. The process of dealing with all of the emotions will, for many couples, mean that it takes at least two years for them to work through their various psychological and personal issues, come to terms with them, and set in place the new relationship.

Unfortunately, children cannot wait two years for their parents to become reasonable with each other. What children need is for parents to be able to at least put on a façade of reasonableness. This would consist of showing some degree of common decency, saying hello and goodbye, not arguing in front of the children, and similar sorts of processes. As will be explained in more detail later, parents need to be able to engage in the 'business' of raising children. It needs to be a joint deal where they put aside their personal feelings and associate only for the task of parenting.

When dealing with the extremes of difficulties in relationship break-ups, I have seen many cases where, in the first year, emotions can be profound, and tensions and problems are of a tremendous magnitude. This has included court action, legal restraining orders and various other dramas. However, a proportion of these couples work through the issues so that two or three years later they have been able to re-establish a workable relationship. The children of such parents will be eternally grateful for the very difficult task the parents have been able to achieve.

Sadly, in the Family Court, I am often asked to assess cases where the Family Court file number may be more than 10 years old. There are some people who are not able to get over the situation and, five or 10 years post-separation, they feel as bitter and hard done by as they did when the situation first occurred. These cases always reflect aspects of the person's psychological make-up. My rule of thumb is; if you have not sorted out your problems and moved on significantly with your feelings after two years, then you need professional help. Early professional help is certainly beneficial, and while people will usually attempt to work through their difficulties as the emotion subsides, ongoing difficulties can become entrenched and need assistance to change.

Children in relationships where the parents have been unable to sort out their difficulties are living in a war zone. In this situation they will feel tension between the parents, have to take sides, take responsibility for the transfer of information, protect one parent's feelings from the other parent and engage in surveillance as a means of surviving. This steals their childhood and takes a tremendous toll on their psychological wellbeing. For the sake of the children, parents who have not resolved the bulk of their difficulties after two years should seek individual psychological help. While they may see themselves as reasonable and their partner as unreasonable – often there is justification for these beliefs – my view is that you can still make peace within yourself irrespective of what the partner may be doing.

Key Points

- Grief over the loss of a serious relationship is a process which runs through a series of stages and usually takes the better part of two years to run its course.
- It is normal to have intense feelings but children need to be spared from the parents' emotions.

- Anger, depression and other emotions impact on parents and children. These conditions need to be managed as quickly as possible. Professional support may be necessary.

- Do not let children caretake the parent's emotions. The parent is the adult, not the child.

- Seek professional help for depression. Mild depression is best helped with psychological therapy. Moderate depression with medication and therapy. Severe depression with psychiatric help.

- Treating your mental health condition is seen favourably by the court. Untreated mental health conditions are problematic.

- "Let's be friends" is a cliché but difficult to achieve immediately. "Let's be business partners" is a more effective approach, where the business is that of raising the children.

Money Matters

Money is a very real issue in the separation process. It is a sad fact that the person who has the greater share of the childcare responsibility when coming out of a long-term relationship will typically end up with the larger share of the financial assets. This is a broad generalisation, and obviously there are myriad legal issues associated with property settlement. For many men, the situation is seen along the lines of having worked hard for the assets while the wife remained at home – but she then walks away with everything.

For women there is also an interesting, and largely unconscious issue, associated with separation and money. At the risk of overgeneralising, many women want protection and security from their partner. During a separation, their security is threatened, and the protector and provider is the person who is now the threat. They may resent their partner for leaving them vulnerable and may seek to restore the balance by having their security returned in dollar value. Women who have this issue to the greatest degree are the ones ho have been full-time homemakers with husbands who have had good incomes. They have lost both their role and their income in the separation process. It is important for women to try to come to terms with their revised role as best as they can. It is also critical men realise that often when a woman is asking for money, she is really seeking security.

While it makes sense that the children are provided for in a property settlement, these are hard issues with no easy solution. In these sorts of cases, the man who is feeling like he has lost everything may well in fact be experiencing reality. He has a smaller share of the children, a smaller share of the assets, a larger share of the financial responsibility and he no longer has a partner. It is important for men in these circumstances to separate out feelings of anger and resentment about this process from the genuine needs of the children. With the increased opportunity for shared care there is a real possibility some men will seek shared care, not in the best interests of the children, but as a means of asset protection.

Women get suspicious of the working father, who at the time of separation suddenly takes a more active role in the lives of the children. There is a body of literature which shows that a percentage of men, who have been limited in their involvement in parenting prior to separation, take on a more active role in their children's lives after separation, and that these changes are maintained about 75 per cent of the time. Therefore, it is critical for men to ask serious soul-searching questions as to whether their motivation reflects a changed attitude as a result of a loss, some desire to protect their assets, or an emotional reaction depending on circumstance. While it is socially quite commendable to want to seek 50 per cent of the children's time, a parent does not need to have that much time for the children to have a meaningful and strong relationship with them. A parent should make sure it is in the children's best interest and not for their own reasons.

Coupled with this issue is whether the parent seeking this sort of arrangement can actually do it at a practical level. There are some people who are self-employed and have the practical and financial flexibility to be able to adjust their hours and standard of living to suit the parenting arrangements. This applies to both men and women. However, arrangements such as "week about" create a very strange circumstance in terms of employment when someone is only available to work every second week. As stated earlier, the priority is to consider the benefits to the child of having a parent available full-time versus spending more time in after-school care.

Key points

- Money is a necessary part of life but do not make money issues cloud your ability to provide for the children.

- Men and women perceive money in different ways and it is important to understand that for women it is often security, and for men it is a fact they are providers.

- For some men, post separation they become more hands on and involved with the children than if they stayed in the relationship.

Trust and Perception

Violence and sexual abuse concerns are issues I am frequently asked to examine as a court expert in the Family Court. There are certainly cases where both violence and sexual abuse are very real issues, and where children are placed at risk or have been directly affected by an abusive parent. However, in the process of separation, one of the fundamental building blocks of a relationship is often destroyed – trust. When a couple is together, they trust each other. When emotions are running high, and trust has been destroyed, parents will often see the worst possible scenario rather than the true reality. By way of a simple example, everyone gets the odd phone call in the middle of the night. However, when in the middle of an acrimonious separation, if the phone rings, the belief is that it must be one partner ringing to abuse the other.

I was involved in a case where the mother alleged the partner was following her. I organised a visit to see the father with the child at a park close to my office. We went to the park and had a successful visit. The day after the visit the mother emailed a letter to my office stating the father was in a blue car, had beeped his horn and had tried to cut her off as she was driving home. In her letter she indicated that she had not actually seen the face of the driver but stated it was him and that he had followed her from the access visit to a turn-off near her home. Unbeknown to her, the father's car had broken down and I had driven him from my office to the visit and had taken him back to my office afterwards. He had been with me for at least half an hour after the visit. In my opinion the woman did not have a paranoid personality disorder, she was simply so distrusting of the father that she perceived all possible situations in the worst light. I do not doubt she was cut off by another driver, but it was a random act of driver stupidity, examples of which occur all over the city each day. In this case the situation had been made worse because the father's behaviour had been less than admirable on some previous occasions, giving the woman grounds to distrust him.

With respect to sexual abuse and the Family Court, I have seen cases from one extreme to another – real abuse to total fabrication. One example where issues of trust were the driving force was in a case where a little girl, aged about 3½ years, made a very clear disclosure that *"Daddy put a snake up my vagina"*. Such a disclosure was extremely graphic. It was coupled with reports by the mother and various relatives of the mother's family that the girl had been extremely distressed after a visit to her father and that it had taken her some two weeks to settle. It sounded like a case where something bad had happened, and that it was sexual abuse.

In the course of my investigation, it turned out the little girl had some sort of urinary tract/bladder infection and had been taken to hospital by the father where a catheter was inserted. One of the ironies in this case was that the father was actually a nurse at the small country hospital and had assisted in inserting the catheter so, in effect, the father had put a 'snake' up the girl's vagina. Because the parents were in a relationship of acute distrust the mother thought the worst. Furthermore, there was no communication between the parents to enable the situation to be discussed.

In my experience as a court expert I have seen the full spectrum of problems. The majority of cases in the Family Court are magnified by the level of distrust between partners and the assumption of the worst-case scenario. In terms of psychological theory, the process underpinning this distrust relates to how attitudes and beliefs are formed and maintained. When people separate, they do not do it because their partner is wonderful, they do it because the partner is awful. When somebody buys a new car, before they purchase the car, there may be several different models under consideration, and there is therefore, considerable psychological uncertainty. Once the person has made their decision, there is justification for the car that has been purchased. The person can see a multitude of positive reasons why the bought car was the best car and why the other cars were considerably worse. The reverse of this occurs with separation where, prior to separation, there is ambivalence. To justify the decision to separate, people's thoughts turn to the worst. It is essential to realise the ex-partner will be viewed through negative eyes until the emotions have been worked through. This can take a considerable period of time.

The psychological name for these processes is attribution and retrospective attribution. Attribution is how we apply cause. If you walk into the room and trip on the carpet, I say you are clumsy which is a personal attribution; you trip and say the carpet was uneven which is a situational attribution. It is how we make sense of the world. When we look back the reasons seem bigger and more justifiable.

Family Break-Up As A Process 49

In cases where parents are concerned about domestic violence or sexual abuse or various other concerning situations, then it is important to seek professional advice from people who have expertise in considering these issues in a separation context. A parent's job is to protect their child and this protectiveness is ingrained to a deep level. However, for an institution such as a court or welfare department to step in, they have to be satisfied that there is an unacceptable level of risk to the child based on the available evidence. Parents seeking evidence can magnify problems, which does damage to the children.

I sympathise with parents dealing with issues where young children in a separation context are raising serious concerns. To act on the basis of unfounded trust puts the child through myriad processes including supervised contact, investigations and questioning. To not act may leave a child in a vulnerable position where abuse is occurring. In Chapter Five I will revisit these issues.

Key points

- Trust is one of the most important variables for a good relationship whether as a couple or co-parenting.

- When trust goes, parents become suspicious and see things from a very negative perspective. Try to make sure your concerns are valid and not simply a projection because you may make false assumptions.

- Issues of domestic violence and sexual abuse warrant special consideration in the lives of separated couples. Do not leave children in dangerous situations, but also make sure you are not overreacting.

2

Developmental Issues For Children

Child Development, Attachment and Survival

One of the most remarkable aspects of the human species is our ability to survive. A feature of both children and adults in crisis situations is the capacity to cope with terrible conditions. Similarly, children create ingenious ways to cope with all sorts of adverse situations caused by parental separation and conflict. However, the research indicates quite clearly that survival is not without a price. There is a psychological toll involved in adapting to difficult circumstances. If you want the best outcome for children, you need to spare them from this toll as far as possible. To best understand the impact of the types of influences associated with parental separation, the starting point is an understanding of normal childhood development.

At the risk of over-simplifying some complex psychological processes, there are two fundamental competing forces which children experience from a very early age. The first of these can be classified as 'secure base' behaviours. These are behaviours exhibited by the child that show us the child feels a sense of inner security because they know their parents will be emotionally responsive when they need them to be. This is not the same as feeling loved but certainly feeling loved is a component of feeling safe. The idea is if the child has a secure sense of knowing the parent will help them, comfort them and make them feel safe, then they will feel free to go out into the world, play and explore all the interesting things around them (which is the second factor). Importantly, this process of seeking the parent for an emotional recharge is how children learn to manage their emotions.

However, if children are seeking a recharge by a parent who is anxious or distressed about the world – often when the child is feeling safe and begins healthy exploration – the parent will call the child back to provide further nurturing. This "over-nurturing" can provide the child with conflicting messages that, "I am here to make you feel safe in the world, but really the world is not a safe place". The idea of 'secure base' behaviours is that children seek a sense of love and safety. This love and safety help them to develop a sense of security.

If children only had secure base behaviours, they would spend all of their time with the nurturing parents and not seek to explore the world. Recharging the emotions is good but once successful, other things need to happen. The second fundamental human instinct is that of exploring the world. Children are created to master the world and therefore seek to leave the safety and security of their parents for ever-increasing amounts of time. With an infant this may be a matter of minutes. The time gradually increases to the point where a typical child in their late teens is ready to leave the nest and explore the world with only occasional contact with their secure bases. Eventually, the child leaves home and is capable of surviving entirely on their own, except perhaps with the occasional call home for mum or dad to send money!

At times of stress, trauma or change, children retreat back to the secure base behaviours and the safe environment. This applies irrespective of whether we are talking about a two-year-old or a 42-year-old. It is remarkable the number of cases I see in the Family Court where, at the time of separation, grown adults return to live with their parents. While there are practical considerations for this, at a fundamental emotional level a large component is the return to secure base behaviours. A child equally seeks the security of the secure base parent. For example, a two-year-old, happily playing with granny, falls and hurts themselves. They only want to be comforted by mummy and nobody else. This completely normal process reflects the fact that while the child may have a good relationship with their granny, their deepest bond is with their mother.

The interesting aspect of such behaviour is that in child development theory, if a child feels safe and secure, then they can put their energies and efforts into exploring the world around them – be that from the beginnings of learning language, through normal schooling, to the complex processes of forming social arrangements with peers. The situation is much the same across the age range, in that secure children can explore the world. Children who are stressed and traumatised will be putting their efforts into seeking reassurance, emotional regulation, and not into their learning and development. Children in a crisis stop progressing and may go backwards.

Linked with the concept of secure base behaviour are the concepts of attachment and bonding. Children develop connections with certain people whom they can rely on psychologically. These are the people with whom the child has an attachment. This person is easy to see at times of stress, but that may not be evident when things are going well. If a three-year-old is playing with a family group, falls over and hurts themselves, they may run straight past the father (with whom they have been actively enjoying a good game) and go to their mother for reassurance. This may be due to the attachment, and it may also be due to learning within the family system that they go to mum – sometimes because she would step in before dad had a chance to comfort the child thus inadvertently preventing his attachment from developing!

The attachment relationship is meant to assist the child in regulating their emotions when the emotions feel too big to manage. Put another way, emotions come without an instruction manual. A child has to learn how to manage emotions. The parent's job is to help regulate the child's emotions so that a child can learn to manage their own feelings. Hence why the child seeks the parent they are attached to during times of distress. If that person is not available, either physically or because of the parent's own issues, then the child does not learn to manage both their immediate distress nor learn the skills they need for life.

The area of attachment is a sub-specialty within the area of psychology. It is also an area where there are critics, and there is some debate as to what the actual nature of attachment is, how it occurs and at what stages. What has been shown without almost any dispute is that where attachment has been damaged at a young age, the psychological implications are profound. The outcome for children who are securely attached is significantly more favourable than for those children whose attachment patterns are insecure or have been totally damaged. This impact relates to adult mental health, emotional adjustment, moral development, and in fact all spheres of adult functioning. The best gift a parent can give a child is secure attachment. On the other hand, juvenile detention centres and adult prisons are full of people who did not get secure attachment when young. (They often also have problems with emotional regulation due to dysfunctions of the brain regulatory systems, e.g. ADHD, but that is a topic for another book.)

There is a fascinating array of literature which examines the child's prenatal connections with parents, particularly the mother. For example, research consistently shows that a newborn baby is able to identify their mother's voice and smell over any other person. The connection to the sound of the mother, and to a lesser degree, the sounds of other key people, is well documented. There is even some interesting research in relation to the theme tunes of soap operas. Where mothers, who are habitual soap opera watchers, sit down to relax and watch their favourite shows, it has been found newborn babies show a calming response when the theme music is played to them. Therefore, there is a prenatal connection to the sounds around them. Obviously, the sound of their mother's voice is present throughout the nine months. Children will also show familiarity to fathers, if fathers have been present. Consequently, there is evidence that newborn children start their lives already with a connection to both of their parents. However, while the mother's voice and sounds will constantly be there, the other influences are variable depending on circumstances.

My observation, as well as my reading of the literature, indicates that children from a young age begin to form their attachments through the familiarity of those around them. Over the first 6 to 12 months, although attachment is taking place, children in general easily pass from one parent to another or one carer to another. During the ages of one through to four, children typically go through stages where they become very clingy to certain carers. It is often, but not always, the carer who is with them for the majority of the time – certainly the carer who is responsive to their needs and is present – and who is able to provide comfort and a sense of calm during times of distress. The literature on attachment speaks of children forming a primary attachment and then a secondary attachment through to multiple attachments as they develop.

Once children get past the age of five, they are quite capable of forming multiple caring relationships. However, the strength and psychological importance of these relationships is generally not as powerful as the connections forged over the first few years of life. It is the early bonds that are the strongest, though it is also the time when things can go most wrong. Too much time away from a primary parent will cause distress, not enough time with the alternative parent will fail to create the necessary attachment.

To introduce you to another concept, bonding and attachment are related but different. The bond is what a parent has with the child. It is built by the parent or carer being actively involved in the life of the child. The attachment is what a child has with the parent. It is built by the parent providing a secure base and meeting their emotional and practical needs. While time with parent and child is part of the process, it is the quality and nature of how the time is spent which determines whether the bond and attachment will grow. Put simply a good parent may not have a lot of time but the child feels secure, and an insufficient parent may have lots of time and never build real attachment.

What is fundamentally important is the fact that the loving relationship between child and parent is not the same thing as the attachment between child and parent. The attachment relationship signifies a function whereby the parent, in their relationship with their child, makes the child feel secure in the world and hence reduces the child's anxieties enough so that normal developmental processes can occur. This parent will obviously have a loving bond with the child. This parent understands the value of limit setting, structure and discipline when needed. They know how to say "No" to their children and know that this still means they love the child.

As a psychologist making recommendations within a Family Court context, I have always sought to protect this early bond/attachment as much as possible because rapid changes at the attachment level is where children will suffer a sense of insecure attachment. For example, a young child, say aged two, who spends too long away from the primary attachment figure, is going to find the experience psychologically stressful, even if they are with a parent who has been considerably involved in the child's life.

There are parents who undoubtedly have a very strong loving bond with their child but because of their fear of the world or their own baggage or pathology, this loving bond can smother or overburden the child and prevent the child from normal developmental progression. For example, the parent who would lay down their life for their child and do everything for their child, and protect their child from making mistakes or facing discipline at school. This then creates the child who becomes a school refuser, has childhood anxiety or develops OCD, conduct disorders, eating disorders, etcetera.

It is particularly hard for some non-resident parents of young children, without an understanding of the attachment processes, to understand how having a little less contact at this time may be psychologically more beneficial to their child's long-term wellbeing. My argument is that when the child is around 3½ to 4 years old, they are quite capable of having an equally strong reliance on two parents simultaneously, but at 12 months through 2½ years of age it may be questionable. One strong, early, stable base is going to be psychologically better for the child than attempting to have two weaker and intermittent bases.

Key points

- Children need to explore the world. This can only be achieved if they feel secure.

- If a child is loved and nurtured by a parent who is anxious or distressed about the world, when the child is feeling safe and begins healthy exploration, the parent will often call the child back to provide further nurturing. This confuses the child and prevents normal exploration.

- The attachment relationship is meant to assist the child to master their emotions when the emotions feel too big to manage. The parent's job is to help regulate the child's emotions so that a child can learn to manage their own feelings.

- If a parent is not available, either in reality or because of the parent's own issues, then the child neither learns to manage their immediate distress nor learn the skills they need for life.

- The loving relationship between child and parent is not the same thing as the attachment between child and parent. Attachment signifies a function whereby the parent, in their relationship with their child, makes the child feel secure in the world and helps them regulate their emotions.

- A bond is the connection the parent feels toward the child. It is not related to attachment the child has with the parent.

- For some children a little less contact with the second parent when younger, may be psychologically more beneficial to the child's long-term wellbeing. One strong, stable base early in life is going to be psychologically better for some children than attempting to have two weaker and intermittent bases.

The Task of Growing Up

When you held your child in your arms during their baby years what did you think about? Were you picturing them as helpless beings dependent on you forever, or were you thinking about what they may become as adults? It is not a trick question to which you answer, "I was so sleep deprived I did not think of anything!" Most people I speak to say they think about the adults the baby may become. The process of changing from a tiny helpless baby to an independent functioning adult is a miracle which unfolds rapidly. As a child matures there are different tasks which the child needs to resolve in order to become that healthy functioning adult we so desire of them.

The task for infants is a mastery of body, gaining a sense of self and an introduction to their sense of security in the world. Up to the age of around four or five children need to be raised within a protective bubble to enable them to safely master the tasks around them before gradually moving into increasingly complex and difficult tasks. This bubble protects them from the problems around them so they can explore the world in measured doses. Sadly, I see care and protection cases whether the children are having too much world at a young age and they are damaged for life. In the Family Court this may vary depending on how protective the parents are toward the child.

In many households there are conflicts between the natural desire to be protective – the inherent desire to focus on secure base behaviours – and parents pushing children to explore the world. This conflict is often reflected in male/female differences. Many fathers are mildly critical of their partners for holding back their children's development by mollycoddling them, while many women experience a sense of anxiety and fear as fathers allow children to try things which are beyond what the mother has deemed the child's developmental level. There is no correct position. I remember when my children were around four years old and I would take them fishing. They would walk around the jetty and never fell in. One time my wife came fishing with us and was saying, "Get away from the edge" to which they replied, "Daddy lets us". My wife realised then they could do it safely. By the same token I took the kids down the big slide in the park only to have them fly off the end and hurt themselves – not seriously but enough to upset them. In the first instance my wife was holding them back, in the second I was going beyond their limits.

Most couples achieve equilibrium in this process, with constant checks and balances between these two primary but necessary directions. In my opinion, erring on the side of caution towards over-protectiveness will probably do no harm and may well do some good. Pushing children to experience things before they are ready might accelerate development marginally but there are risks and costs in this approach. On the other hand, there are certainly some parents who are so protective that children may fail to develop normally.

When these differences occur in a separation situation it is grounds for potential psychological concerns. A woman who has been in a relationship with a partner who has a tendency to push the children to explore the world, becomes extremely anxious about what might happen when the children leave her. This fear is possibly grounded in reality, however, chances are there is an element of over-protectiveness kicking in. The father, on the other hand, becomes critical of the mother's tendency to hold back the children. There are no simple answers to this problem other than to recognise that these are common fears and anxieties, and that both parties need to be sensitive to these issues.

As children move through the ages of 5 to 11 their primary focus is absorbing large amounts of information from the world around them. Here they will learn vast quantities of information, both of an educational nature and in social spheres. You see it in the children copying parents in the kitchen, garden and garage.

Children in this age group have quite limited abstract reasoning. By this I mean they tend to learn by rote and imitation rather than thinking for themselves. How much do you hate seeing the same movie or clip again and again because the child likes the repetition for learning? A simple implication of this is that for children through this period, one parent is right and one parent is wrong. It is not possible for both parents to be right.

Similarly, over this period, there are significant emotional differences in how children cope with situations. From the ages of six to eight children often, in a separation situation, have significant sadness. Children in this age group have come to rely on the security of the family structure and interpret the changes to the structure as a collapse of their entire protective environment. Their emotional immaturity causes these children to feel extremely sad because they cannot protect themselves from their sense of loss.

The latter half of this developmental period, 9 to 12 years, has been called 'the age of anger' by some writers. It is during these ages that children feel a sense of resentment and anger at the changes caused by the disrupted relationships. This anger escalates because these children live by a rigid code of ethics or rules. Situations are black and white, and they are unable to understand there are two sides to the story. Unlike younger children, who fight feelings of anger towards a parent, these children are active in expressing their hostility to the angry parent.

The anger and discontent felt by girls around the age of 10 are among the most hostile reactions I have seen in children who are living in separation conflicts. Interestingly, it is often the particularly bright children, who are seeking to understand the world but lack the capacity to process the information, who are most extreme in their anger. They may direct their feelings with intense anger to the other parent and, in so doing, express all the righteous indignation of a disgruntled princess.

Sadly, there is a small percentage of parents who, rather than seeking to moderate this anger, actually turn the anger against the other parent. This increases the alienation between the child and that parent and achieves short-term gains through revenge. However, unless this anger is successfully resolved, children of this age are going to suffer significant and permanent problems. The alliance forged between the parent and the child at the age of 10 or 11 is a weapon which turns against the parent as the child moves into their early adolescence. Pumping hormones into a system of pre-existing anger is akin to pumping petrol onto a pre-existing fire. The reactions are spectacular and the damage devastating.

Children from broken families in both younger and older age groups, who show symptoms of sadness and anger for shorter periods of time, are perfectly normal in their grief. This is how children need to deal with grief. The issue becomes a problem when they become stuck in their sadness and anger. As a rule of thumb, if these periods last longer than one to two months, there is probably a need for some professional intervention by a child psychologist. Getting professional help early should be considered where the intensity of the reaction is extreme.

If you remember earlier in the book I wrote children cope best with separation between the ages of 7 and 12. I hope you can now see what I meant by saying that these are years not without their difficulties – it is just that the difficulties here are shorter and less profound in the damage than at some of the other age points.

As high school begins, there is another marked psychological transition in a child's development. Here the need for independence and the opportunity to make decisions for themselves becomes increasingly important. However, this capacity is based on pseudo maturity. The child thinks and believes they are mature, but it takes the next 10 years before they become truly mature. Recent research in brain development has indicated that it is not until age 26 that brain development has reached its optimal structuring. It is only when we are in our mid-20s that we have the capacity to truly analyse and understand the implications of what we have been through.

Key points

- In any household, there are conflicts between the parents' natural desire to be protective (the inherent desire to focus on secure base behaviours) against the desire to push children to explore the world. The balance is even harder to achieve when parents separate and do not communicate.

- Children under the age of 12 years lack abstract reasoning. This means their brains are not equipped to allow them to see both sides of a story. One parent is right and one parent is wrong. It is not possible for both parents to be right. Never put a child in a position of having to understand who is to blame.

- Around the ages of six to eight, children will most commonly manifest emotional problems as sadness while children aged 9 to 12 are more likely to express anger.

- Teens have a pseudo-maturity but do not have full maturity until their mid-20s.

Decision Making Capacity in Children

At 13 years a child considers they have the maturity to be able to decide for themselves and work out what is best for them. Sadly, I also find parents arguing we should go with the children's wishes because that is what they want. At this age they are certainly more capable of making these decisions but this is within the limits of being a 13-year-old. To understand what I am talking about, consider how you would write your will. If you had $2 million of assets, would you let your 13-year-old have unlimited access to that money if you died, or would you have the money held in trust until they are older? How old? You are legally an adult at 18 years. What would you have done with the money at that age? When I wrote my will, I actually made 25 years old the age at which my children could access their portion of the will. Most people would agree that it is not until adulthood that we should have the right to make decisions. Even then, major decisions, like investing a large sum of money, require life experience. Unfortunately, too many young children may be asked to make decisions that will profoundly affect their future at a time when they are inadequately equipped to make such life-changing decisions. They can tell us what they like but they do not have the capacity to tell us what is best for them.

I am frequently faced with parents who argue a child should be allowed to decide what is best for them. I remember an example where, during a home visit in a Family Court case, a four-year-old was asked by their mother if it was all right for mummy to take the toy off the table for lunch. The child said no, we all had to eat lunch on our laps! This type of independence does not socialise the child, and in my opinion is a recipe for creating a precocious child who will not fit in with others. I am not saying children should not have rights, I am saying they come unsocialised and parents have an obligation to train children how to be responsible adults.

To understand a child's decision-making process, consider the example of placing a bowl of ice cream and a plate of dinner before children of different ages. The typical three-year-old will eat the ice cream, and would not have understood that they should have eaten their dinner first, unless it is an overly enforced rule in the house. The typical eight-year-old would know that they should eat the dinner first, but will probably eat the ice cream anyway. By the time a child is about 14 or 15 years old, you would hope they would choose the dinner before the ice cream. In other words, young children know what feels good, while older children are increasingly able to determine what is best for them. As stated earlier, my view is that it is not until we are in our mid-20s that our brain is developed enough to truly decide what is best for us. Therefore, the concept of 'the views of the children' in the Family Court is a dicey one, unless the views are seen in a developmental context.

In the teenage age group, however, the dilemma which parents face is that this is an age where it is critical for children to learn how to make decisions for themselves. Children of any age need to have some input into what is happening in

Developmental Issues For Children 67

their world but, for older children in particular, this needs to be explained more fully and carefully. The point is; a healthy parent knows that to explain and discuss does not necessary mean to give what the child wants.

Judith Wallerstein is one of the most widely known researchers in how separation affects children. While there have been some criticisms levelled against Wallerstein's research, some of her findings have been quite profound. One finding which is relevant at this point was that 80 per cent of pre-school children were not told by their parents that a separation was going to take place. They just woke up one morning to find their parents separated. With older children the statistics were a little better. However, given that the whole task of parenting is to gain independent, thinking, functional adults, appropriate involvement of the children in aspects of the process is important. Obviously, one does not ask the child permission to separate from the other parent. However, to ensure that children have a sense of control over their world, their involvement in the process is important.

Children as young as two years old can have a simple explanation of things which are going to take place so they can understand what is happening. For example, "Daddy has a new house and will be sleeping there, he will be seeing you soon." Obviously, the primary school and teenage age groups need significantly more discussion.

Once families are in the court system there may be orders made which prevent a parent talking to the children about what is going on. This is helpful in stopping negative input but it also makes no sense from a developmental point of view. Children need to know what is going on. The key is what they know and the parents' capacity to be big enough to be mature about it. I once asked a little girl what daddy called mummy and she said, "cheating f...ing whore" (mum had an affair and the father caught them in the act). When I asked what it meant, she said, "I don't know but the way he says it is not very nice".

Coupled with this process is the fact children have a tendency to believe they may be responsible for what has happened with their parents. Probably the age where this is at its highest level is in the three to eight-year-old age group. Here, children have a very egocentric point of view. They believe they are the centre of the world. For example, a four-year-old at the zoo hears the lion roaring. They may say, "Why is this lion roaring at me?" As an adult we know the lion is not roaring at the child, it is just roaring. This same logic is applied to parental separation. Why are mummy and daddy breaking up, it is because of me!

As explained earlier, younger children tend to learn through a greater degree of imitation and copying, while older children learn through thinking and reasoning. In normal development, younger children need exposure to healthy role models, both male and female, whereas older children need healthy discussions with different male and female role models. On top of this, the gender of the child becomes an issue. There is research to indicate that boys are more likely to seek and need greater contact with their father, especially during adolescence. Many tribal societies have a transition from living with mothers to going to fathers as a rite of passage. In my own family, my children have had times when they go more to mum or more to me in terms of general factors or for specific things. It is not simple and having two parents and other trusted helpful adults ("the village") is going to give the best outcomes. The problem is that in a complex separation one or other parent becomes a gatekeeper which restricts the normal ebb and flow necessary for children to get their needs met.

The Judith Wallerstein research also showed that in the first year after separation, girls recovered a lot better than boys. Boys often got worse in the year after parental separation. At the five-year mark, boys were often still doing much worse than girls and were more likely to be showing significant learning and social problems. Ten years after separation, the situation actually changes, with boys showing an improvement in their overall adjustment and girls becoming the more psychologically vulnerable group, particularly as they enter into early adulthood. As they moved into adulthood, girls were afraid they would end up marrying men like their fathers and were concerned about problems associated with that. Do you get the message what this research is telling us? The impact from separation is a lifelong process which is tremendously complex. It is profound that changes are being noted at 10 or more years post separation.

This section clearly highlights the fact that parental separation is an action that takes place in a complex melting pot of factors. The needs of children are many and varied and change with time and developmental progression. Each child is uniquely individual in their capacity to cope and deal with the difficult task of making sense of their experiences. They will bring the total of all aspects of their development to the recovery process.

Key points

- Children need an age-appropriate explanation of what is happening in their lives and they need to be able to express their views. Never lie to children about what is happening but make sure the truth is age appropriate.

- Too many young children may be asked to make decisions that will profoundly affect their future at a time when they are inadequately equipped to make such life changing decisions.

- Avoid letting children make the decisions. It should be the parents who know best.

Coping Options

As stated in the opening paragraphs of this section, my observation is that children are ingenious survivors. It is both sad and unfortunate they have to survive the aftermath of separation because the cost of survival will be debited against their ability to explore the world and master developmental tasks.

Some issues will be developmentally related. For example, I have witnessed situations where problems at handover have been continuing for months. The young child (typically around 2½ years) is upset about their visits with the other parent and angry on return. I have observed handovers where the situation is extreme, with the child not wanting to go on contact. They resist by hiding under chairs, holding onto doorframes or a parent, and crying hysterically. I have then gone – within 10 minutes of the child leaving the office – to see the child at the other parent's house. This previously hysterical child is now happily playing as if there was never a problem.

This reaction begs the question; What is going on? Within the circumstance of distrust associated with Family Court action, the father blames the mother for alienating the child. The mother blames the father for being abusive or hurting the child. However, what is usually but not always being played out here is a child who has a strong single attachment and is becoming distressed at leaving. It does not normally reflect the quality of the relationship with the other parent. The child is generally fine once they are with the other parent. What it does reflect is that the child is leaving the primary parent for a period longer than they can cope with. Usually, this situation will pass by the time the child is a little over three years old. Unfortunately, where parents have been fighting in court for ordered visitation, they are extremely reluctant to reduce time with the child to allow them to re-stabilise and re-establish secure base behaviour. The really sad aspect in these cases is that there is often a precipitating event. For example, the child suffers an illness and, at the time of being sick, needs to be with their secure base parent, but is forced to go on contact. Being forced, the child then becomes anxious and unsettled and the other parent becomes a trigger for separation.

I would further add that after the first visit goes wrong, a cycle of problems builds. The child remembers that last time they were upset so going next time they are already distressed. In simple terms, if something is pleasurable or negative our brains are designed to remember them. If something was negative, then we avoid it next time. Now the child may be getting upset for no reason other than having to do this makes them upset.

The 10-year-old who angrily refuses to go on contact is likely to be coming from a very different psychological position. It is not a developmentally related issue associated with attachment.

This child is typically bright, thinks in black and white terms, and is unable to cope with an independent view, so they take sides. They are not the anxious child who is worried about being separated from the primary base, but the determined child who wants things on their own terms. They also can get locked in the power and control issues – they refused to go last time so they are refusing again.

If the conflict in the child's life is severe enough, then ultimately the child has only a few ways of coping. They either have to take sides (fight or flight), or they have to be robust enough to duck beneath the conflict (avoid) and get what they need from both parents, or become paralysed in the middle (freeze response).

Taking sides can have all sorts of interesting implications. I had a case which was all about refusal and unless you have seen this it is hard to believe it is actually possible. The mum said the child was refusing to go to dad and when made to go, came back upset. Dad said the child was asking for more time with him. I had four-year-old Jessie come into my office with me while her mother was in the waiting room. As we drew pictures together, I asked if she would like to see her daddy, and Jessie said to me yes she would love that. I then asked if she would like to sleep over, and again she said yes. She even said she would like to be able to sleep over on the weekends. It was totally the opposite to what mum had been telling me that Jessie had told her. Perhaps dad was right after all.

Immediately after our 30 minutes of chatting together Jessie went out to the waiting room, put her hands on her hips and said to her mother, *"I told the man I never want to see Daddy again."* Shocked, I pulled her back into my room and said, "Hey sweetie,

I am confused, you just told me you want to sleep overnight for weekends but now you are saying you never want to see daddy!" With all the wisdom of her tender years she said, "But mummy gets upset if I tell her I want to stay at daddy's house". What a beautiful example of survival. The little girl was telling her mother what the mother wanted to hear, while telling me what she really wanted. Sadly, she has worked out to say what people want to hear and was managing her mother's emotions. She could just have easily been telling daddy she wanted to sleep over so as not to upset him but in this case it appeared genuine.

There is almost nothing more psychologically scary for a younger child than the fear of the loss of their primary attachment figure. In an older child, who has two very strong attachment figures, the separation creates a conflict in a similar manner. In the examples given above, neither child has developed adequately enough to deal with the issues, nor have solutions for dealing with this internal conflict. At the end of the day, they will align both consciously and unconsciously with the one person they perceive will provide the greatest degree of love and safety.

In the cases where the child has a strong relationship with two dominant parents, they may find their ways of coping by ducking beneath the conflict by saying what they want the parent to hear, or saying nothing. I have also seen a small number of children who have very strong relationships with both parents and both parents are telling them different things. They end up not trusting either adult. That is a terrible plight, and hearing a little person say, "I don't know who to believe, so I trust no one", is pretty profound.

Where there has been a tendency in the family system for there to be a dominant parent and a minor parent, the child does not have to choose in the same way. Those decisions, in many respects, have already been made. A normal child who has a good pre-existing relationship with both the mother and father, faced with a conflicted separation situation, is going to struggle. The greater the struggle for loyalty, the more it forces children to take sides or develop other coping strategies, such as telling parents what the parents need to hear.

The sort of strategies used by the child is going to depend, in part, on the conflict and also on their personality. In the psychological research literature there have been debates as to whether personality is created or innate. As a father of twins, I would argue most strongly that children are born with their individual personalities. This may be shaped through their various experiences, but there is no question there are some children who are stronger willed than others. In particular, the dimensions of emotional sensitivity are an important consideration. There are some children who cope readily with change and are emotionally able to deal with the world around them. In the psychological literature they are sometimes said to be the "easy temperament" children. Other children tend to be more reserved and take longer to "warm up", the so-called "fussy temperament" children. In particular, these children are the ones who are going to have the greater difficulty coping with the separation situation.

I have seen normal children, who are not in a conflict, fearful of leaving their parents. I remember my brother at the time he was seven or eight years old getting homesick and having to come back in the middle of the night from a sleepover at a friend's house. Fortunately, he did not have to experience parental separation and enforced contact visits but, if he did, he would have had a really hard time dealing with the situation.

A final important consideration to be raised at this time is the issue of a child's experience of both objects, as well as people, providing them with a sense of security. Children from a very young age will turn to objects such as a favourite teddy, or a jumper that mum gave them, to comfort themselves when they feel anxious, sad, etcetera. I had one smug father say he did not need anything to come from the mother's house as he had exactly the same things, including the same bed and teddy bear. Their three-year-old son put the father in his place by saying the teddy smelt different so it wasn't the same.

Places can provide this same sense of security for the child, but the familiarity in a place can only develop over time. Continuity and constancy provide familiarity. Therefore, children do best in familiar environments. I remember the first time I took my children camping, when they were aged three. We went to a most beautiful camping place and, after setting up the tent, they spent the entire afternoon in or around the tent and were totally unwilling to go off and explore. They were extremely excited about going camping. They were extremely happy to be there, but it was simply too overwhelming to take in more information than the novelty of the tent. It was not until the fourth overnight camping trip, and another nine months of development, before they began to leave the tent site and explore some of the other places around them. Similarly, when we went on holidays with them at the ages of three and four, the first couple of days were typically spent in the holiday house before they began to explore the beach, parks and other activities around them. This is simply a reflection of the need for security. When they are at home, they are happier to explore.

In a parental separation situation, the introduction of overnight contact creates issues for children. The child may be away from not only the primary parent but also their familiar environment. This can cause quite a sensory overload, particularly if the other parent is not sensitive to the fact the child needs a while to establish safety and familiarity with their environment.

Simple factors such as allowing a child to take favourite toys or objects with them on visits are a way of helping them maintain continuity. As pathetic as it may sound, and as ridiculous as it becomes in some cases, there are couples who have needed court orders to determine which objects and items have to go with the child and be returned afterwards. There should be no need for court orders to determine whether a child should be allowed to take a teddy bear or toy from one home to another. Common sense and a love of the child should allow the child to have whatever they need go with them and return later. One parent explained they kept the toy as a reminder of the child when they left. While that is touching, in whose best interest are they acting?

The bottom line is that the more sensitive the child's disposition, the more important the continuity of home and objects becomes for that child. The easy-natured child will cope better, but the sensitive child will need more support to cope.

To put this chapter into perspective, ultimately there are only five ways children can cope in a conflict. These are shown in the diagram below.

Developmental Issues For Children 77

1. There are two ways of ducking beneath the conflict. One way is to tell the parent want you think they want to hear as Jessie did in the example.

2. The second way to duck beneath the conflict is to tell the parents nothing. It is easy to do and is frustrating for the parents. The child never says what they did at the other parent's home.

3. Some children, because of their nature, are able to speak their mind and say what they want. However, this is not easy because children spend their lives being told what to do by their parents. Therefore, the idea they are free and able to express their view is not always a safe assumption.

4. If children have enough pressure, or they have a strong relationship with a particular parent, taking sides can be easier than the conflict. I have also found that if conflict goes long on enough, eventually, children end up taking a side as a way of ending the conflict. Taking sides can be for survival purposes – fear of losing the love of a parent. It can be manipulated by alienation as in the case of "thing" referred to at the start of this book, or it can be realistic estrangement because the child does not get on with the parent. The aligned child is a complex situation and professional help early is very important.

5. Having no sides is the example I gave earlier. It is sad to see children who cannot trust either parent.

Survival of children in conflict

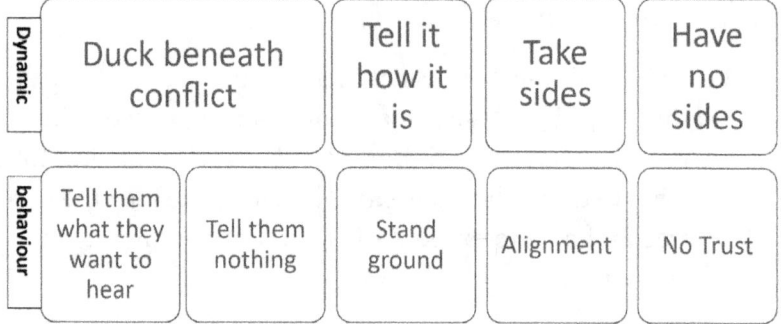

Key points

- The young child, typically between two and three years old, may get upset about visiting the other parent and may be upset and angry on return. What is commonly being played out here is a child who has a strong single attachment and is becoming distressed at leaving. In other words, the issues for very young children are often attachment related.

- Older children, if the conflict is severe enough, have only one of two ways of coping. They either have to take sides, or they have to be robust enough to duck beneath the conflict and get what they need from both parents.

Developmental Issues For Children 79

- The child who ducks beneath the conflict may tell parents what they want to hear or may say nothing at all. The child who takes sides reacts angrily about the visits as they are unable to manage the differences between the parents.

- If the conflict is intense, psychological survival means the child has to align both consciously and unconsciously with the one person they perceive will provide the greatest degree of love and safety.

- Objects, such as teddies, clothes and blankets, may provide children with a sense of security. Children from a very young age will turn to objects for comfort. Be sensitive to the child's need for comfort objects.

- Familiar places bring a sense of security for many children. Ensure changes are gradual and children have a chance to adapt to the new environment.

Managing Change

An important but often overlooked aspect of how attachment and developmental factors impact sharing arrangements is the need to make incremental changes which allow the children to adapt and consolidate that change. Children take time to adapt to a new regime, whether it is time with a separated parent or even going to a new activity.

I argue that it takes around six cycles of time with a changed arrangement before it feels like the new normal for the child. For example, a child of two years old starts having a sleepover with the other parent for one night per fortnight. The first visit may be exciting. However, once the reality is experienced, it may have felt overwhelming, so next time the child is more reluctant, or even defiant, about going. From my observation a developmentally normal child of easy temperament typically takes around six cycles for the new arrangement to be the new normal. Therefore, any reactions are possible in the first few visits, but you know the child is adapting when the problems diminish toward the end of the time. If you do the maths, six cycles of a fortnightly pattern is about three months.

A child with a fussy disposition, or special needs like autism, intellectual disability, or anxiety, may take longer than six cycles to stabilise into the new normal. They should be closely monitored for adaptation as they have less capacity to cope when things go wrong. If they are not getting used to the situation by the time six cycles have occurred, it may mean there is a problem which needs to be addressed. Unfortunately, if it is based on court orders there may not be flexibility to change the schedule quickly enough to meet the needs of the child.

Once the new normal is established, it then needs to be consolidated before making an increase. In most cases, six cycles of the new normal allows the child to be comfortable prior to the next change. Therefore, adding nights to the arrangement for a young child, or changing school holidays into larger blocks, may take six months or more for the child to feel like they have adapted enough for the next change.

Smaller changes may need less adaptation and consolidation, bigger changes can take even longer to get used to. The critical variable is that a child who is adapting is going to need secure base behaviours, while a child who is consolidated can explore the external world. Changes which are too quick keep the child in a state of needing comfort and security.

Developmental Issues For Children 81

I like to err on the side of conservativeness when it comes to attachment. There have been interesting studies, such as in the 1940s, when psychiatrist Lawson Lowrey began to study hospitalised children and noted that children placed in foster homes were showing high instances of "hostile aggressiveness, temper tantrums, enuresis (bedwetting), speech defects, attention demanding behaviour, shyness and sensitiveness, difficulties about food, stubbornness and negativism, selfishness, finger sucking and excessive crying". Hospitals in this era had a belief that children got upset when parents went home so to stop the upset, they banned parents from being with the children. Some parents reported that after just two weeks in hospital the children were never the same on their return home. We would now call it attachment damage, and most children's hospital these days have facilities that allow the parents to stay with the children to prevent this. If the time away from the primary attachment figure is too long, children may be damaged.

Perhaps this can help you understand why incremental building of time, with adequate adaptation and consolidation is so important. A little less rush may result in a better functioning child, and in the future create a more capable adult. There needs to be a scaffolding of attachment built around the child to enable them to cope. It is important to remember that time alone does not build attachment but experiences – where the parent can help regulate the child's emotions – is what builds attachment. The parent is attuned to the child.

In line with the chicken and egg arguments, which comes first, the time or attachment? The answer to this is easier than the chicken and egg scenario. Attachment must come before time. However, time is still necessary for attachment. If time does not increase attachment will not grow much. What has to happen is the time should be extended toward the upper end of the child's current ability so they can adapt and then consolidate. If it is more than their ability it creates attachment issues. If it is not enough, the relationship with the second parent will not grow.

Key Issues

- Attachment must come before time. However, time is still necessary for attachment. If time does not increase attachment will not grow.

- When building arrangements in the post-separation period, time needs to be extended toward the upper end of the child's current ability (but still within their limit). They will adapt and then consolidate.

- Exceeding the child's current ability will result in many symptoms of attachment disturbance.

- To consolidate an arrangement, my rule of thumb is it takes six cycles for something to become the new normal.

- Once the child has adapted, a minimum of six cycles is necessary for consolidation. Consolidation is necessary so the child can get back into the exploratory mode of being, otherwise they are constantly seeking secure base comfort.

3
Parental Factors

When it comes to parenting, I am of the opinion there is no such thing as neutral behaviour. Everything a parent does has an impact. That impact will either help develop the child's potential, be it intellectual, psychological, social or emotional, or it will have a negative impact on the same dimensions. Most of these impacts are like an artist's brush on an oil painting – there may be the odd stroke which is powerful in what it does to the picture but mostly it is a composition made from hundreds of tiny bristles. Each little stroke may seem insignificant but the multitude of strokes creates the picture. The combination of the very significant lines with the tiny imprints builds the picture.

So it is in a child's life. Their future may be shaped by several big actions but mostly it's the composition of thousands of little actions over time. Positive comments, supportive interactions, reasonable challenges, secure base experiences or overcoming difficulties all add to a child's wellbeing and development. Stressful reactions, feelings of anxiety and uncertainty, change, negative comments, trauma, and put-downs likewise are cumulative in the negative direction.

As an adult, therapy can help add colour to a dark picture, perhaps overlaying some of the dark legacy. However, my contention is that the underlying picture remains indelibly imprinted. Therefore, my biggest single caution for parents at any part of the parenting process, but particularly through separation, is that their behaviour will have a tremendous impact upon their children's lifelong adjustment. They must paint the best picture possible with all the tools and knowledge they possess.

As explained in the earlier sections of this book, the impacts of parental separation are not a short-term crisis but are an enduring legacy that shapes the child's future. Children from broken families have bleaker outcomes in almost all respects, be it the likelihood of drug addiction, criminal offences, broken marriages, suffering from depression and so forth. As will be explained further in the book, it is not the separation per se which does the damage but the conflict and how the parents act that determines the damage. The power is in the hands of the parents. Unfortunately, the bulk of the power is in the hands of the most pathological parent because the other parent cannot do anything about it.

From a psychological point of view, I find it fascinating that it is not the separation alone that has the impact, but the way in which the parents deal with the situation that has the biggest influence. For example, research shows that parents who, five years after separation, have not resolved their difficulties and still have significant animosity, will have a far larger impact on their children and their children's psychological future than those parents who resolve the difficulties. The effects are cumulative and dependent on the parents' ways of interacting.

The whole point of this book is to highlight that parents do have a choice. Separation will impact your children – the degree of impact will depend on the choices you make in dealing with your former partner and children.

When one considers the functioning of the family, it is important to consider it is a system made up of interactions between various people. Therefore, in the simplest case, separation impacts on two parents and one child. The nature of each parent and how they deal with the situation, plus the personality of the child, are the determining factors. Start adding in other children (stepchildren, half-siblings to new partners), different personalities, blended relationships as parents commence new lives, and the system changes with each addition. The way in which the extended family, such as grandparents, cope and act adds yet another dimension of impact.

When we talk about separation, we are implying it is the separation of parents. However, it is also the separation of families. You can choose your partner but you do not choose your in-laws. At separation, they will have reactions, feelings and impacts on the children. Often grandparents are the ones funding the litigation. They may be influencing the children in negative ways. They may be the voice of reason trying to smooth the rupture. They also have relationships with the children which will change post separation. It is necessary for you to control your family in the separation process. What was once a loving extended family splinters into two tribes. Tribal warfare is going to hurt the children.

The most marked example of children responding differently within a family system came to light when I saw three children in a situation of a highly conflicted parental relationship which had been going on for years. The couple had been separated for seven years and over that time the difficulties had continued at an intense level. The oldest boy, aged 11, lived with the father and was refusing to see the mother. The oldest girl, aged nine, lived with the mother and was refusing to see the father. The youngest boy, aged seven, was willingly visiting both parents on a rotational basis. In this particular case, the outcome was not simply a product of the parents' behaviour but an interaction between the personalities and natures of the children and the way in which the parents were dealing with the situation. However, the point I make is that it is the parents' responsibility to deal with the situation maturely. The children do have a right to act childishly; the parents do not.

In the separation literature, amongst the worst possible scenarios for the psychological adjustment of children are situations where parents either consciously or unconsciously force children to align against the other parent. There is a major controversy within the profession with respect to this subject. Richard Gardner, an American writer, proposed a concept called 'Parental Alienation Syndrome'. He described how children under certain circumstances reach a point where they not only don't want to visit the other parent, they become extremely preoccupied with the denigration of that parent and align completely with the resident parent. He described this phenomenon as taking place in the absence of domestic violence or sexual abuse, so it is not a product of fear (in those cases it is not considered Parental Alienation Syndrome). It is also only considered to be Parental Alienation Syndrome if the pre-existing relationship between the now despised parent and the children was previously positive. In other words, there was a prior relationship of a seemingly positive nature.

Critics argue heavily why Parental Alienation Syndrome should not be accepted as a syndrome. Arguments include such concerns as the lack of published literature, inadequate research, that it is not actually a 'syndrome' and so forth. The arguments against it being a syndrome are well founded as it does not meet a diagnostic criterion and the nature of the dynamics accounting for alienation were flawed. The arguments in the profession and community are hostile and vicious. It is still one of the most controversial areas in the whole child custody litigation domain throughout the world.

My views are best illustrated by a comment made during a trial by a very experienced Family Court judge when the debate about Parental Alienation Syndrome was being raised and challenged. In the middle of the trial the judge turned to the various solicitors and said he had been sitting on the bench for 25 years and had seen dozens of cases where children do not want to have anything to do with the other parent, long before anyone ever called it Parental Alienation Syndrome. He said he did not care what it was called as he had no doubt the situation really takes place. The bottom line is that children can and do take sides to extreme levels in some cases. We cannot find the correct terminology for it because alienation is now a heated word some consider to be politically incorrect. Professionals tend to use terms like "resist and refuse dynamics" in the literature even though parents call it alienation.

As time has passed, the research has tended to concentrate on the fact that it is a system problem, with the actions of the mother, father and child contributing to the circumstances. In one of the worst cases with which I was involved, two children had not seen their father for nearly three years due to a variety of reasons including having been enrolled under false names in a different town after the mother had left the father. The only possible arrangement that could be brokered was for the children to see the father for an hour a year, to give them the opportunity to express any change of view about seeing him. On the first visit the children arrived with dark glasses and personal alarms. On subsequent visits they came with various strategies such as computer games to play to avoid eye contact with the father. The sad aspect from my perspective was that when the children came to see me, they readily and willingly spent the preview period sharing various aspects of their schoolwork and general positive life achievements, but when the joint visit commenced, they were completely silent for that period of time. Until the children each reached their 13th birthdays the visits were repeated annually with absolutely no change.

The only aspect that showed any change was that the children shifted from being fearful to mildly contemptuous of the father's actions. For the most part they said absolutely nothing. I encouraged the father to persevere with the visits for just one reason – one day the children will reach that point where their brains are developed enough to have abstract reasoning and they will have to ask the question, *"Why was this man willing to be treated that way each year, year after year?"* There would be only one reason, and that is because he loved them.

The psychological implications from these children's alienation will probably take decades to be fully apparent. Both children were academic high achievers and were generally coping well with life. Therefore, one could argue they did not have a need for the father. On the other hand, one wonders about how they will cope when it comes to their own intimate relationships, with the model of avoidance, the learning of disrespect, the inability to deal with life conflicts, lying about their identities, the lack of healthy male role models and so on. When these factors take their toll, I suspect the psychological implications of their situation would become more evident. The literature shows that the psychological implications of such cases are often severe psychological damage.

As a general rule, children shift in their alliances between parents at different times. There are times when children want more female input from their mother, and other times seek those aspects their father can offer. Adolescent boys, in particular, need alignment with male role models. Research has indicated that boys raised in households with men tended to be less aggressive than boys raised in single-parent homes headed by women. It is likely the male role model and learning to manage rough play assists in the management of aggression.

In cases where parents have had an amicable separation, it is extremely common that as children reach their mid-teens they often desire to live with the non-residential parent – the grass always seems greener on the other side of the fence. I would argue that probably two-thirds of these children do it for a period of anywhere between three to twelve months and then return to where they have always lived, while the other third actually find it a more suitable arrangement for them at that time of their life. Sometimes, mothers do not cope as children reach their teens, so they send them back to their fathers for him to "handle" the problems. The shift toward living with fathers is reflected in the statistics cited earlier which showed the proportion of children living with their fathers increased with age, especially during the children's teenage years.

In my opinion, where parents have put forward barriers to this normal ebb and flow of relationship, such as through conscious alienation attempts, they will one day pay the price. This will be when the children reach sufficient maturity to see both sides of the story, be that at 13 years old (when abstract reasoning commences) or 26 years old (when their brains finish developing). At that time they will turn against the parent they perceive is blocking their relationship with the alternate parent. Therefore, in my opinion, there are short-term gains for the obstructive parent when they turn children against the other parent, but in the long-term the outcome is negative.

Even in cases where the other parent may be hopeless, inadequate or have some significant failings, having small doses of reality can be helpful to the children. The reason for this is that at a simple level, all of us have two fathers and two mothers. The first parent is the real parent and the second one is the fantasy ideal parent we create in our minds based on our image of what a parent should be. Children who do not have access to the real parent only have the ideal parent as the fantasy they create in their mind. Therefore, if a parent is hopeless, children safely exposed to this over time gradually come to see the flaws, for example, parents who break promises and who do not follow through. While this is disappointing at the time, it is a reality-based experience which helps them prepare to manage it in the future.

An interesting experience I had was with a child not wanting time with their parent. When I asked him why he said this he said, "Dad will arrive late, spend ten minutes sorting the car out, want to take me swimming and I don't like swimming so I will sit and watch, then we will go home. He doesn't know me or care." When it came time for the visit, that is exactly what happened. Dad was late, had nowhere for him to sit, and wanted to go swimming. There was no connection between dad and boy. Similarly, I saw a girl who played Aussie Rules football with a passion, a passion she shared with dad. Mum liked girlie things and wanted her to do modelling and was not taking her to training. In end the girl went to dad's house. It was a better match.

I would like to point out that children not wanting to see a parent due to family violence may have a justified reason to not see them. However, in care and protection where children are exposed to sometimes very high levels of abuse and trauma, they often feel ambivalent rather than negative about the abusive parent. Sometimes they want to align with them as they are the powerful one, so it makes sense to please the powerful one.

I hope you can now see that a child not wanting to see the other parent is not simply a case of alienation or not. It is complex as to why a child may not want to see the other parent with many reasons for it, varying from direct influence of a parent, factors in the child causing them to align, and a host of social variables around personality and circumstance shaping the situation.

Finally, I would like to note that if a child does not have access to this parent, they miss out on the benefits the parents may bring and the child creates a fantasy of what they may be like. If that fantasy is false, based on the parent being evil or harmful, it is damaging. Also, when the time comes, they may seek that parent out but the only way to get there is by burning bridges because they have not been allowed to seek them out previously. This then makes it hard for them to return. Therefore, in my opinion, even if your ex-partner is hopeless, small doses of reality are better for the children in the long-term than total avoidance. Children are quite perceptive and will gradually build their own understanding. I qualify this by saying the first priority is to ensure children are safe, and it is therefore important they are not exposed to inappropriate risk if they are to have time.

Key points

- There is no such thing as neutral parenting behaviour. Everything a parent does has an impact. That impact will either help develop the child's potential, or it will impair, inhibit or damage it.

- It is not the separation that has the biggest impact upon the child, but the way in which the parents deal with the situation. The better the parents manage the situation the better the child will adjust.

- Parents do have a choice. Separation will impact the children; the degree of impact will depend on the choices a parent makes in dealing with the former spouse and children.

- The worst possible scenarios for the psychological adjustment of children are situations where parents either consciously or unconsciously force children to align against the other parent. Do not play the child against the other parent for any reason.

- It is extremely common that as children reach their mid-teen years they desire to live with the non-residential parent. Parents need to understand this is normal and should not feel like they are a failure.

- It is common that children who have been prevented from seeing the other parent, will turn against the parent they perceive is blocking their relationship upon reaching their mid-teens.

- Even if the ex-partner is truly hopeless, small doses of reality are better for the children in the long term than total avoidance. Children are quite perceptive and will gradually build their own understanding. Of course, safety must be paramount if a child is exposed to an inadequate parent.

Parental Behaviours

While there is a small percentage of parents who actively seek to alienate their children from the other parent because of their own personal pathology, the majority of people I see are responding to mistaken beliefs and assumptions about how the world works. There are numerous things parents can do with the best of intentions but which have a long-term negative consequence in terms of relationship factors. I will discuss some of these factors in the following section.

A starting factor is 'the truth'. There is a complex issue associated with helping to inform children about what is happening. In my opinion it is absolutely critical that neither parent lies to their children. In the long term, children discover lies and then become disillusioned about parental integrity. Some of these situations can come about with the best of intentions.

In terms of my own experience, when I was in my late teens I found out my parents had previously been married to other people and I had older half-siblings living in England. When one considers the circumstances of the situation, in the late 1950s or early 1960s, separation was a rare event with a lot of social stigma attached to it. My parents immigrated to Australia, in part, for a new life, so they thought they were acting in our best interests (relative to that time). They also felt that not speaking about the situation would be in our best interests. However, upon accidentally finding out about my half-siblings, my initial reactions were intense shock and disbelief about my parents, particularly in regard as to what else they may have 'lied' about. I felt I could not trust any part of my family history because I did not know what may or may not be true. These implications show it is important to ensure children have a reality base to work from.

However, in family break-up situations, the opposite problem can have an extremely dire consequence. Parents who tell the children too much "truth" about what is happening are placing their children both at risk and in a psychologically dangerous situation. Too much information forces children to take sides. A four-year-old does not need to know that "mummy is having sex with a new man", as I was informed during one assessment. Fortunately, when I asked her what "sex" meant she could not tell me, but she did know that it was not a good thing for mummy to do.

Consider, for example, explaining to a four-year-old a situation where there may have been domestic violence. One mother may choose to say: *"Your father forgot to use his words and used his hands instead. I'm not going to stay in the home with him because using his hands hurt me, and he needs to learn to not use his hands."* A second mother in a similar situation may choose to say: *"Your father is a bad man who hits me and he is dangerous and might hit you too."* A third mother may choose to say: *"Your father is a fucking arsehole who's good for nothing but beating up women and children."* All three of these examples are comments parents have said to young children and the children have remembered it to repeat it back to me. All three are 'the truth' as seen in the situation.

The first comment will help the child have a sense of reality about what had happened but will enable them to establish some sort of relationship with both parents, while understanding that the father does have a problem which needs help. The child in the second example is going to have a negative view of the father and may be fearful. The third comment will not only induce a negative attitude but the mother's actions will cause a moral corruption of the child's wellbeing.

There are other possible scenarios associated with the example given. A child may be told that nothing happened and that the parent is leaving because, *"Mum and dad don't love each other anymore."* In that particular case, if a child was aware of the fighting between the mother and father (and there is a good chance they will be), then the child's reality is being denied, and they are not learning to express emotional issues. The child may also wonder when mum and dad will stop loving them.

Whether a child is aged four or 15, it is critical they have a sense of the reality of what is happening. However, that truth needs to be age appropriate, considering their developmental needs and maturity, but also delivered in such a way that the child is able to maintain some healthy balance with both parents.

The model I use is what I call layers of truth. What you tell a four-year-old, 10-year-old, 16-year-old, and 26-year-old should be different. However, the core needs to be consistent. The domestic violence example used earlier is a good example. At four, using hands not words are useful things to say and is still true at 26 when mum says she was a victim of domestic violence and had to leave. Think of the truth being shaped like an upturned funnel. As the child gets older the funnel gets wider with more truth and detail.

In a perfect world, shared truth is important. As explained earlier in the book, many children do not even know their parents have separated. The best parents have agreed to what they will tell the children and share the language and expression of it. They may have even received professional advice on how best to explain it to the children.

Key points

- Never lie to children about what is happening as it discounts their experiences and results in them learning not to trust you.
- Children need to understand what is going on so they can make sense of their world.

- Truth is helpful for a child but the truth needs to be age appropriate and not damaging. Layers of truth revealed at different ages are important.

- Parents who tell the children too much "truth" about what is happening are placing their children at risk of psychological harm. Too much information forces children to take sides against parents they love.

My Time with the Children

During the 35 years I have been assessing families for the court, I have come to the point where hearing the words *"my time with the children"* triggers me quite heavily. If it were not ethics and professional behaviour restraining me, I feel like yelling at them *"no, you have it all wrong!"* The parent who says *"It is my time with the children"* typically shows a pattern of beliefs and behaviour which are the total opposite to what children need.

Underpinning *"my time"* is a sense of rights; *"It is my right to have time with the children and during that time I will do what I like and no one will be able to interfere with my time."* I frequently hear it in cases where the child may have an invite to a birthday or sporting activity on that weekend, and the parent says they will not take the child because it is happening in *"my time"*. The person guards their minutes with the children with a sense of ownership.

In a similar vein, parents calculate the hours and if, for some reason, there needs to be a change, those hours need to be debited and credited for make-up time. To be perfectly clear, I have no problem with the concept of make-up time if someone is on a restricted time schedule. For example, if a parent only has six hours supervised time a week, for some reason if that time is reduced, they should be entitled to have the balance of the time. However, I was involved in a case where the term-time ratio was 60/40 and the court order said the father had half of the school holidays. Rather than changing the residence at a set time in the middle of the holidays, if the school had an extra day or two for teacher training, public holidays, or other purposes, the father would move the start point of the holidays by half of the extra time, including one pickup at 8pm at night. The concept of swings and roundabouts in life had no meaning to him. The time was determined to the minute and determined now.

The healthy parent does not say *"It's my time with the children."* The healthy parent says, *"It's the children's time with me."* While this may seem like simple semantics it essentially completely changes the dynamic, in that the purpose of the time with the parents is for the child's benefit, and that child should then have the right to time with both parents, with both parents catering to the child's needs and what is best for them. If the child is invited to a birthday of a friend, then they should go. If the sport they like to play is run on Saturday afternoon, then take them. If the handover in the school holidays is more practical earlier, then make it convenient for the children.

A simple example from the Family Court was one where the children did junior surf club until 11am on Saturday with a hand-back time of 12 noon. The mother lived near the surf club, the father 30km away. After the surf club he would insist he drive the 30km home with the children, shower them and then put them out for the mother to collect. The mother would pick them up and drive the 30km back. For the sake of an hour the kids could have been spared 60km of driving and two hours of dead time.

I believe the child has a right to a safe, meaningful and healthy relationship with both parents. I do not believe that arrangement needs to be specified by the hours and minutes involved but by the quality of life it is going to enable the child to have.

Of course, there are parents who will sabotage time with a parent by deliberately encroaching on the children's time with the other parent, and that can be as bad. For example, a mother who had the children doing three different activities on the weekend which she insisted the father take the four-year-old child to. At least two were not necessary for a young child to do on the weekend.

The best way to implement this is to simply ask yourself, is this proposal best for me or best for my child? The healthy parent will choose what is best for the child, the selfish parent is going to choose what is best for themselves. That does not mean that you simply do what a child wants, but what is going to help create the best well-rounded adult. It is also what will build a co-parenting relationship between yourself and the other parent.

Key points:

- *"My time with the child"* is about rights of a parent. Children need what is good for them not what is good for the parents.

- *"The child's time with the parent"* is a mature and healthy way of considering the situation.

- A parent who will sabotage time with the other parent by deliberately encroaching on the children's time with that parent can be as bad as the parent counting minutes when they have a decent block of time.

Overburdening the Child

The four-year-old in the domestic violence scenario may have been a boy. If the mother said something along the lines of, *"Your father is dangerous, you need to protect me,"* then the mother is expecting the child to fill a role that a parent would normally have filled. There are many different forms this situation can take, but basically where a child is put into a position of looking after a parent's practical or emotional needs, they are being inappropriately overburdened.

An earlier section of this book described the emotional process of separation. It is common for conditions such as depression to occur and for parents to regress in their psychological functioning. In other words, they function as a younger person. It is not uncommon in families where there are older children, that the depressed or regressed parent relies on the child in a role reversal. This can sometimes be explicit. *"You're the man of the house now"* or *"You're a big girl, you need to help your mother"*, or indirectly, such as a busy parent relying on the 10-year-old child to prepare meals.

This process psychologically overburdens children who are required to take on too much responsibility for their stage of growing up. It prevents them from being able to be children and often leads a child to fend for themselves. An only child, or eldest child, is particularly at risk as they are most likely to become the parent's ally or confidant in these situations. The term sometimes used is the child becomes "parentified". This is a very unhealthy place to be for a child.

The use of the child to meet the emotional needs of an adult is a psychologically devastating aspect of the separation. This can come about inadvertently. For example, a depressed father, who has a very limited friendship network, sees the children on the weekend and spends most of that time crying and saying how bad he feels – the children then have to tend to the parent's emotional needs. These children then feel a sense of responsibility for their 'poor father'. In the process they may start to blame the mother, or they may start suffering anxiety and avoidance because they are unable to deal with the intensity of the emotional reactions. The mother may have a similar scenario which can overburden a child due to feeling helpless and powerless. If it is a migrant family sometimes this can be even more complex where they need the children to interpret language for them.

To protect the children, the situation should be reversed. The healthy parent should be able to keep their emotions under control and allow the child to express their feelings. However, when everyone is sad, depressed or angry, it becomes increasingly difficult to hold feelings separate from the child. I am not saying that children should never be aware of parents having emotions. They can learn to deal with emotions if they see their parents successfully dealing with emotions. However, it needs to be in very small doses and the parents need to explain how they deal with it.

Another form of this situation occurs when a parent says how much they will miss the children when they are not present. *"I'll be thinking about you every minute you're not with me, and I will be very sad until you come back."* This may well be a true statement, however, the child then feels they are responsible for the parent's feelings. The healthy parent would say words to the effect of, *"I'm going to miss you over the coming week but I've got lots of activities to do to keep me busy, and I will feel very happy when I see you again."* It is about packaging emotions to make them more child friendly.

When children are distressed, it is not uncommon for them to climb into a parent's bed for comfort. Most parents give them a cuddle and some comfort, and then put them back into their own bed. During separation, children will frequently end up staying in the parental bed. The parents need to ask clearly and honestly; Is this taking place because the children need it, or is it because the parent needs it? I appreciate that co-sleeping is something some parents choose to do, and certain cultures do it a lot more than it is done in Australian families. However, the issue is whether it is for the child's benefit or for the parent. In particular was it happening before separation? If not, there is a good chance it is about parental need or convenience. It needs to be handled but with appropriate expertise.

One of the most common situations which arises in a separation process is a person's feeling of emptiness at nighttime – particularly sleeping alone in a double bed when, for the past 15 years, they have been sleeping with someone else. The child in the bed helps ease that pain. However, the child is being used to fill the parent's need. Being responsible for parental comfort will prevent the child from learning to be independent. It also stifles normal development that takes place when children sleep in their own bed.

In saying this, I am not referring to cases where parents come from a background of, or a belief in, children sharing beds with parents. There are some families where children do this for a number of years. What I am speaking about are cases where the children have previously slept independently but who are now regularly sleeping in the parent's bed, particularly if the parent is putting them there, rather than the child coming into that bed in the middle of the night. I would like to add that children going through separation often have sleeping issues and will wake more often. However, they need to learn to self-regulate (so they can get back to sleep themselves) than be comforted to sleep otherwise they will always require comfort and not learn self-regulation.

Key points

- When a child is put into a position of looking after a parent's practical or emotional needs they are being inappropriately overburdened. Let the child have a childhood and not grow up too early.

- The use of the child to meet the emotional needs of an adult is a psychologically devastating aspect of separation. The healthy parent should be able to keep their emotions under control and allow the child to express their feelings.

- Parents who say to the children how much they will miss them when they are not present can cause a child to feel responsible for the parent's feelings. It is okay to miss the child but do not let the child feel responsible for that feeling.

- In separation, children will frequently end up staying in the parental bed. It is critical to determine if it is for the comfort of the parent or whether the child really needs it. Healthy parents give them a cuddle and some comfort, and then put them back into their own bed.

- Mentally healthy children can put themselves to sleep when they wake. During separation they may need help to learn how to do this again.

Loyalty Demands

During the separation process, emotionally healthy parents are able to accept the children have feelings towards both parents. Parents who are struggling emotionally demand loyalty from the children and put them in positions of taking sides. This is something which may well have been occurring in the relationship prior to separation, as it is quite common in people who lack psychological maturity themselves. They perceive the relationship as a competition. Getting the child's love is seen as part of that competition. For example, saying to the child, *"Tell me who you love the best"*, *"Am I your favourite"*, or playing games such as, *"You don't want to sit on his lap, you want to sit on mine"*.

In a separation situation these loyalty demands can become a very bitter conflict. *"You like your father more than you like me."* Children in these situations are put into a terrible predicament because rejection from the loved parent is every child's worst fear. Within this context I have seen cases such as that of the four-year-old girl saying in my office that she would like to sleep over at her daddy's house but who then walks into the waiting room to tell her mother in a loud voice, *"I told the man I never want to see daddy again"*. This is a child who has loyalty concerns and, in particular, is aligning with the mother (because the mother, in this case, is the strongest emotional attachment figure).

Loyalty demands show up when children are asked to keep secrets. *"Don't tell your mother I've got a new girlfriend. This can be our little secret."* I was involved in a very sad case of two normally high-functioning parents. One of the parents had inadvertently set up this type of "loyalty demand" process for years. He spoke about how he had been having 'private time conversations' with the children and that these 'private time conversations' were between him and the children – they did not have to tell their mother they were having these conversations. This was before separation and was used to discuss the mother's "inappropriate" behaviour. While I think it is fantastic to debrief children in their rooms before sleeping, it should not be to undermine the other parent.

At a more extreme level the same father had also taken the children for psychological counselling to deal with their issues, but *"without their mother having to know"*. He saw himself as acting in the children's best interests because he said they would not have gone to counselling if they were aware their mother knew it was happening. However, this sets up a difficult dynamic for the children in that they are in a position of loyalty to their father against the mother.

Another form of this problem comes about when parents talk about their feelings in a way which implies blame. For example, "*I still love your mother and we could be a family if she came home*", or alternatively, "*I love your father but he hates me*". This creates a sense of one parent being the cause of all the problems. An even worse thing to do is to get the child to do the work for you; "*Please beg mummy to come home.*" In some cases, it may be true, in other cases it may be manipulation, but a relationship break-up is never that simple, and it will not help the child to be placed in the middle of this conflict. It is acceptable to say, "*Mummy and daddy don't get on at the moment but we both still love you.*"

At the most basic level, putting children in the middle sets up an 'us' versus 'him or her' dynamic. The same type of parents often speak about 'we', meaning 'the children and I', when referring to situations. In this case it was the 'we' versus 'he or she'. 'We' have decided what will happen. In this particular dynamic the needs of the children are so entwined with the needs of the parent that the child is forced to take sides.

It should not be a competition to be the best parent. One of the unfortunate aspects of Family Court processes is that it forces parents to prove they are the best parent. It then becomes complicated for the children when they are encouraged to support the parents' case. It may not be as black and white as that, but some children are dragged into the situation to a level where this is the outcome.

The solution should be simple: be the best parent you can be and do not worry about what the other parent is doing. You can only control what you do. The research tells us children notice what their parents do and as adults they can tell us who was supportive and who used to badmouth the other parent. Therefore, if you want your children to respect you when they are adults themselves, it is important you start by being a good example while they are young. It is made easier if you remember you cannot have too many people love your children.

Key points

- Emotionally healthy parents are able to accept that the children have feelings towards both parents. Parents who are struggling emotionally demand loyalty from the children and put them in positions of taking sides.

- Loyalty demands show up when children are asked to keep secrets from the other parent. Do not have conversations with a child and then demand they be kept confidential.

- Do not compare feelings in a way which implies blame. Similarly, do not talk about who could fix the family break-up.

- Be careful about the language used to describe relationships. Words like "we" can refer to "the children and I" versus the other person. It then excludes the other parent.

- A child cannot have too many people love them.

Show of Emotions

If I was asked by a client how to turn a child against a parent, for ethical reasons I would choose not to answer. However, the answer to that question could include elements of two main strategies. The first strategy is to denigrate the parent and say how bad, how awful, how terrible they are. This strategy may or may not be successful.

The second strategy would be more subtle. It would relate to emotional reactions. For example, when the telephone rings, the mother would slap her hand on her head and say, *"Oh, it's that terrible man again"*, or if the children ask their father if they can go and visit their mother, he says, *"Of course you can visit your mother again, if you really want to. I don't know why you would, but if you really want to, I'm sure I'll cope while you are gone, and I wouldn't worry TOO much"*. By emphasising the emotions of anxiety or sadness, it hooks into the child's loyalty concerns.

The success of this strategy will largely depend on the child's personality and development. The pressure is intense, and they are going to have to decide who to align with. For example, a child in the 9 to 12-year-old age group, who is already feeling angry, is far more likely to align with the angry parent.

The psychological cost of these strategies is that they induce a sense of guilt, fear or anger. As these feelings develop, and then get projected onto the other parent, damage is being done to the child's psychological wellbeing.

The human brain is amazing. It has the cortex which is logical thinking and the limbic system which is the emotional system. The cortex is under conscious control, but the limbic system reacts. Therefore, while I say manage your emotions it is easier to say it than do it for many people. If you are saying nasty things, it is the logical brain and you can stop that, especially if you address the anger which is driving it. If you are reacting in front of the kids, then it is probably more unconscious factors coming from the past or from your limbic system. That requires you to do some good therapy to lower your triggering response. A type of therapy called Eye Movement Desensitisation and Reprocess (EMDR as it is known) is really good for addressing triggers. EMDR is described in more detail elsewhere in the book.

Key points

- Do not express in detail to the child how sad or angry you are about a situation. Your job is to regulate the child's emotions, rather than for the child to regulate your emotions.

- Emphasising the emotions of fear, anxiety or sadness hooks into the child's loyalty concerns. In doing so, the child aligns with the parent. It is important to keep the child out of the parents' emotional state.

- If you are triggered, try doing EMDR therapy with a trained psychologist to lower your reactions.

The Rights of the Child

A factor commonly intertwined in Family Court proceedings, creating problems for children, is the parent's perception of the rights of the child.

To illustrate, I have often heard a parent say: *"My child does not want to visit their father and there is nothing I can do to make them."* I then ask how old the child is, and they reply *"Four years old."* In such cases it makes you wonder who the parent is. During a home visit I once conducted, the children had been doing some artwork on the kitchen table when the mother asked the permission of her four-year-old twins to take their paintings off the table so we could all have lunch. One of the children said 'no' so we ended up having our lunch on our laps! Apart from my astonishment at the fact this parent had not established any sort of authority role within her home, it suddenly made me realise why she had been unable to get the children to visit their father. In this particular case it was her failure to adequately parent the children.

I believe that children have rights. They have the right to be informed about what is going on, and they have the right to have input into decisions which affect them. However, the whole point of parenting is that children start life without any inherent morality or socialisation. The parenting task is to help socialise children to enable them to fulfil their intellectual and emotional potential and to fit into society. Therefore, the amount of weight one would place on the decisions of a four-year-old should differ greatly to the decisions of a 10 or 14-year-old.

Using schooling as an example, there are often occasions when children do not want to go to school but parents act in the best interests of the child by making them go to school. They usually try to find out why the child does not want to go and then seek solutions. They do not simply respect the child's decision not to go. However, in a parenting conflict a parent may turn around and say it is the child's right to decide whether to go or not. They should be troubleshooting the problem not acquiescing to the demands of a child.

In a separation situation, the hardest aspect for many children is the transition between one home and another. Therefore, they often need a little push to go to the other home, but once there, the children function well. I remember times when my children were engaged in a fun activity and I asked them if they wanted to do something like go to the park and have ice-cream and they said no as they were immersed in what they were doing. A while later they wanted to go to the park. Therefore, the children's rights and wishes need to be viewed in context. Once the Family Court is involved, and court orders are in place, there is often no choice in the matter. It is important children do not believe they have the right to decide whether or not to see their father or mother. *"It's up to you to decide if you want to go ..."* This is unacceptable and inappropriate for younger children in these circumstances.

Statements such are these become increasingly appropriate for children in their upper teenage years as they have an increased capacity to decide what is good for them and they have enough maturity to make an adequate assessment of the situation for themselves. Furthermore, it is very hard to make an angry 14-year-old do something they do not want to do. Until that time, it is important children are dealt with in a 'no fuss' easy-going manner, but with a firm "not negotiable" stance.

There are international rights of children (Convention on the Rights of the Child or CRC). These make for interesting reading and are important for the wellbeing of children. They recognise the importance of children having the right to express views, but they do not say children necessarily have the right to determine what is best for them.

In my opinion, if you want to raise responsible children, they need to understand how to make decisions and have input into the outcome. However, they do not need to make the decisions about everything. Giving a child the right to choose between parents is a lot of responsibility which carries with it heavy burdens. In my opinion, the greater the conflict the less input into the outcome the child should have.

Key points

- Children have rights. They have the right to be informed about what is going on, and they have the right to have input into decisions which affect them. However, they also have a right to be a child. Parents have a responsibility to act in the best interests of the child not simply on what the child wants.

- Using schooling as an example, there are often occasions when children do not want to go to school, but parents act in the children's best interests by making them go to school. The parents do not simply respect the children's decision not to go but try to fix the problem. The same should apply to visits with the other parent.

- The hardest aspect for many children is the transition between one home and another. Therefore, they often need a little push to go to the other home.

- Until a child is truly old enough to decide for themselves (mid-teens and onward), it is important they are dealt with in a no fuss easy-going manner, but with a firm "not negotiable" approach.

Parental Communication

Parents need to be able to raise children in an effective manner. How parents conduct themselves in dealing with their children's issues will have a tremendous impact on the children's wellbeing. It will be much better for the children if parents are able to put aside their issues and act in a co-operative fashion.

Children also observe parental behaviour closely, either positive or negative, in this regard. For example, a child who requires their soccer boots while visiting their mother, will form a negative view of their father if their mother is willing to get the boots but the father is not willing to hand them over. This, at one level, gives the children a lot of power because they can play their parents off against each other. On the other hand, there is also the reality that the parents need to deal with any issues between them.

In this day and age of modern technology there are numerous avenues available to parents to communicate without having to use the children. The worst possible scenario is to make children become messengers to co-ordinate events and issues. Asking the child to, for example, tell the other parent to return a particular item, or relaying other sorts of messages, is simply not appropriate. With SMS, email, mobile phones and numerous parenting Apps, parents have a number of ways in which they can communicate in a non-emotional manner to ensure these very important functions are achieved.

In the Family Court, where conflict may be high, parents are often advised to have a "communication book" or communication app. This is a book, transferred with the children's bag from visit to visit, where the business of parenting is put into writing. As long as the book is used as a mechanism for dealing with issues, it can be a highly effective way for the parents to communicate. However, some parents use these books to continue to put down the other partner. It is particularly unhelpful to write in the book comments such as, *"Please pay the school fees you stingy bastard"*, or *"Hey stupid, don't forget the swimming lessons this week"* (as I have seen written in some communication books). Furthermore, a father who puts a wedding photo of his new wife and family on the front of the book is being either insensitive or provocative. The books are for the parents to deal with parenting business, it is not a book for the child or a forum for parents to continue to undermine each other.

I would argue that communication books are an outdated mode of communication and parenting apps have a much stronger place in the lives of modern families. Ones like Our Family Wizard has a tone meter which tells parents that their tone could be seen as aggressive. There are also free apps and apps with different features. What you want to ensure is that they respect your privacy and are secure. Free ones have to make money somehow and you need to ensure your material is not shared with others.

The children will benefit if their parents can show at least a modicum of decency in the communication process. If they can talk politely, courteously, simply smile and say hello, it will mean a lot to the children. Young children will often say to the parents, *"You must come and see my new bedroom"*, or *"Come and see the piece of work I've put on the fridge"*. These sorts of things may be very difficult to achieve but if parents explain in simple terms to the child that, *"Mummy and daddy live in different houses now and it is not proper for daddy to come into mummy's house"*, children will often accept these comments.

To look at the issue from the children's point of view, what they want is a return to their old life, with two parents who can relate to each other. It is completely normal for children to want to reconnect their parents, and they do not understand why their mother and father cannot talk to each other or be nice to each other, particularly as the parents have told them to behave that way with their friends.

If a child has had a fight with someone at school, their parents do not usually tell them to be mean and nasty or refuse to talk to that person for the next few years. Most parents try to teach their children strategies for resolving problems, and yet children witness their parents not doing this. In my opinion, this is ironic and hypocritical.

The worst possible outcome in terms of communication is for parents to become verbally or physically aggressive. This becomes an extremely scary experience for children. Parents are supposed to be the secure base to go to. Parents are supposed to be the people who provide calming responses to problems when children feel distressed. If communication between parents becomes aggressive which the children are exposed to, it increases their uncertainty and anxiety. If either one or both of the parents are unable to cope emotionally with each other, the use of third parties to organise exchanges is preferable to the children seeing their parents getting upset.

Communication extends to being able to be present at important events, the school or sporting clubs. Two parents who can stand next to each other and be polite will be great for the children's confidence. Parents standing at the opposite end of the field, who will not let the child talk to the other parents as it is not "their time" are causing damage to the children.

Key points

- The way in which parents communicate when dealing with their children's issues will have a tremendous impact on the children's wellbeing. Children need parents to put aside their issues and act in a co-operative fashion.

- The children will benefit if their parents can show at least a modicum of decency in the communication process. Create the illusion of friendliness by talking politely, being courteous, simply giving a smile (it is free) and saying hello. It will mean a lot to the children.

- It is critical not to let children become messengers to co-ordinate events and issues. With apps, SMS, email and mobile phones, parents have a number of ways in which they can communicate in a non-emotional manner away from the children.

- Where communication is poor, parents should consider having a "communication book". This should be for the parents to deal with parenting business. It is not a book for the child or a forum for parents to continue to undermine each other.

- If either or both of the parents are unable to cope emotionally with each other, the use of third parties to organise handovers is better than the children seeing their parents getting upset.

Parents Doing Really Badly

As a forensic psychologist the Family Court will appoint me in cases where severe problems occur, particularly cases where there is major parental alienation, sexual abuse or domestic violence allegations. In the years I have been working in the system, I have seen cases from one extreme to the other. There are cases where children have been sexually abused, or where a partner is extremely physically dangerous to their spouse. There are cases where major mental illness impairs a party's functioning, or where people's personalities are such that they actively and maliciously seek to destroy the relationship between the child and the other parent. This book is written to only overview those sorts of cases, and more importantly, help explain the positive strategies which may benefit children.

Extreme cases require professional advice of an expert nature. In saying this, I would offer the following caution when seeking advice from mental health professionals; there are many excellent psychologists and psychiatrists who are brilliant clinicians within the scope of their normal practice, but ill-quipped to understand the nature and dynamics of these cases. Children in the Family Court are an area of special expertise. Some of the problems are unique and, if not handled expertly and with due consideration of the legal ramifications of certain courses of action, can inadvertently make the situation worse for the parents and child. If you are in this unfortunate circumstance, research carefully from whom you will seek professional advice. Contacting the counselling service of the Family Court, the family law section of Legal Aid, or other agencies that deal with the family matter in court, are good places to start the research.

While I am not going to detail the management of these problems, I would like to offer observations of some things I have learnt from these hard cases. The first of those observations was described in an earlier section, and that is prior to separation, people have a positive filter of their partner's behaviour – post-separation they have a negative filter. This is the standard psychological process of life. Human nature is such that we have protective biases or filters that justify and rationalise our decisions. At times of separation, trust is at an all-time low. Therefore, in many cases, seemingly normal behaviour becomes interpreted with an extremely negative slant.

For example, in the area of sexual behaviours, young children can be sexual in their nature, language and behaviour. Young children like to explore their private parts (little boys will touch their penises whenever they can, it is not uncommon for little girls to masturbate), while young children will occasionally grope the breasts of women, say rude things they have heard, and so on. The task of parenting is to socialise children from doing these things in inappropriate ways. If the child's behaviours occurred within a context of trust and communication between parents, most of this behaviour can be explained through discussions in that context. Some of these may become the future funny stories told at 21st birthdays – "Remember when you asked the lady on the bus how the baby got in her vagina!" Or, "Do you remember when little Marcus was in the bath, he did a wee on his sisters head." Unfortunately, if a child goes on a visit to a despised ex-partner and comes back displaying the same behaviour as that parent, consideration may be given to the worst-case scenario as a first option, triggering expensive, stressful and comprehensive assessments.

In allegations of sexual abuse in particular, comprehensive assessments, where younger children are involved, often return equivocal findings. Family Court criteria consider the case in light of unacceptable risk, often leaving everyone in a no-win position. The parent who has raised the claim is left in a situation where the risk has not been completely removed, the accused partner has not had his or her name cleared, and everyone has been through a very stressful process. The reason for this is that the court is of necessity evidence-based and often the evidence from young children is quite equivocal.

In a situation where a child says or does something of an inappropriate nature, I advise parents to seek good advice (both legal and psychological) before embarking on a comprehensive assessment and, indeed, even before raising the allegations. It is particularly important prior to commencing any action, that parents talk to an objective third party about the allegations to work out whether the parent's own judgement has been clouded due to feelings of distrust.

The most common problem I see is the inappropriate and repeated questioning of children when a possible allegation is raised by the child. Parents are not trained in forensic interviewing and often do everything wrong. They repeatedly ask leading questions. My advice if a child makes a disclosure is to ask as little as possible to determine if it is serious or not, just note what they say. Write it down promptly. Get professional help. Too much interviewing contaminates the information the child is giving you.

By the same token, the need to be sure about an allegation has to be weighed against the fact that the more contemporaneous an investigation is, the more likely the process will reveal solid evidence. In the life of a child under five years of age, allegations can fade within weeks of the event without prompts or reminders. Prompting leads to counter allegations that the parent who raised the allegation of abuse is influencing the child. It is also important the child is not repeatedly questioned about the issues raised, as questioning can cause leading, or contamination of, the child's thought processes. This tainting does not make a situation less true but it can cause the assessor of the issue to have doubts about the source of the information. In cases of heavy questioning, there is evidence children can be led to make false allegations. Carefully, but not in view of the child, note what the child says (verbatim if possible). Quick but careful actions are necessary if young children of separating parents raise sexual abuse concerns. However, unless the evidence is fairly strong, the outcome is not going to be helpful.

Family violence is another area of concern. There are some initial comments in this section, and because it is such an important topic, further analysis is provided in the following section. There is a well-established body of literature that shows children living in significant domestic violence situations have many serious psychological problems as a result of these experiences. However, determining what constitutes significant domestic violence, and weighing up the impacts on the children, can be a problem.

The first consideration is that the context within which the violence has been taking place has to be determined. Longstanding relationships, where problems have only emerged during the high stress of break-up, are very different to relationships which have had ongoing sustained difficulties. The emotional nature of separation, often involving depression, sadness and anger, can cause people to be reactive and irrational.

This does not justify the behaviour but it does explain why there is a problem, and it often means the issues will be transient. A year or two down the track, these problems may be resolved.

The second important consideration is to determine whether the actions of the aggressive partner are predatory by nature, or whether they can be viewed within the context of common couple reactions. A simple example to highlight this is the case of a woman who claimed her husband was violent towards her. When I asked her to explain the situation, there were two incidents of physical violence. The most serious incident occurred during an argument. The husband had said he had enough of the argument and was leaving the house. She pursued him as he left the house. As he started to walk off the front veranda, she threw a cup of hot coffee down the back of his neck. He swung around and hit her in the process. While she accused him of family violence because he hit her, her actions could also be classed as violent. It is not good for children to see such displays, however, the actions of both parents are at a similar level of intensity and they are each triggering the other. Post-separation, it would be preferable if these two people do not spend time with each other until they can control their emotions.

The likely risks to the children would be very different in a case involving another man I saw who was at one point arrested for hiding in the ceiling of the woman's house, slashing the car's tyres, burning her clothes and sending letters with threats to kill her. These actions are not the result of equal reactivity of two people whose emotions are out of control, but of someone imposing their will upon the other due to significant issues of control. These issues are not going to go away without restraining orders, legal intervention and significant therapy.

Once again it is a question of objective judgement as to whether the issues are being clouded by the emotion of the situation, or whether they represent a serious risk. I believe most strongly that children should not be placed in situations of unacceptable risk. Their safety is paramount. However, the parents need to make an objective assessment with respect to the real risks, rather than base their judgement on their feelings towards the other person.

Irrespective of the nature of the situation, children are worse off where they see their parents being physical towards each other. Many children will relate such incidents for years. These are not actions that children are likely to forget.

An important consideration is the parents' belief about whether the children have been exposed to the violence within the home. One study asked women, who were leaving a domestic violence situation to go to a refuge, whether the children were aware of the violence. While about 50 per cent of women believed the children knew about the violence, when the children were asked, 90 per cent were aware. It is important not to kid yourself about whether children are aware of the violence or arguing. Children are astute observers and probably know a lot more than you think they do. We used to accuse our children of having "long floppy ears" when they were listening in on conversations which they should not be listening in on.

Children do not see cause and effect in the same way as adults. For example, there is the issue of one parent provoking the other to the extent where the other parent hits the provoking parent. Younger children who witness this get very confused because they often get angry at the parent who has been hit because they saw them "start it". As a parent, you spend a lot of time asking your children, "Who started it?" Now your children are applying those principles to you.

Key points

- If you are in the unfortunate situation of a very nasty separation, research carefully the professional you will seek advice from. The impact of separation and court proceedings on children is a specialist area where expert knowledge will help (while ill-informed professionals may make the situation worse).

- A parent should talk to an objective third party about their concerns relating to sexual and other abuse in order to work out whether the parent's own judgement has been clouded due to feelings of distrust.

- Talking to a child about abuse issues is a specialist skill. It is important the child is not repeatedly questioned about the issues raised, as questioning can cause leading or contamination of the child's thought processes.

- If concerned about possible abuse, take good notes of what a child says about the situation, including what you asked and what the child responded. If possible, do not write these notes within view of the child.

- Do not show your emotions to the child, even though this may be a very distressing time for you.

- Where separation is involved, I strongly advise parents to seek good advice (both legal and psychological) before raising allegations of sexual or other abuse. While the safety of a child is paramount, badly handled allegations will involve children in major investigations for no beneficial outcome.

- There is a well-established body of literature that shows children living in significant domestic violence situations have many serious psychological problems as a result of these experiences. These issues need to be effectively addressed.

- It is important not to kid yourself about whether children are aware of the violence or arguing. Children are astute observers and probably know what is going on even if you have not told them anything.

Family Violence

Family violence is a topic which has gained a lot of publicity in recent times, and for quite justified reasons. Family violence is toxic in its impact on the parties involved, and children, in particular, suffer many problems when exposed to family violence. The research shows it is not separation which harms children but conflict. Family violence makes conflict worse, so it ramps up the impact on children.

Law has always recognised family violence as a risk issue, but in recent times has increase its focus and the amount of weight it will place on allegations of family violence. As a worker within the family law space, I have observed two effects from this increased focus and increasing legislative weight. The positive benefit is it is putting the protection of victims of family violence, and especially the children, at the forefront of decisions around the long-term care of children. It is enabling early identification of problems and allows for management of the issues. How well it is able to do this may be debated, but there is no debate that it is being dealt with in a more proactive way and given greater status in the decision-making process. I have seen cases of extreme risk, where properly addressing the issues is certainly easier and more effective now that it was 30 years ago. It is now taken seriously.

However, because family violence has now become a trump card in parenting decisions, I am also seeing an increase in the labelling of minor behaviours as family violence. Everything is being interpreted through a family violence lens. Sadly, this does a disservice to those people – typically women and children but also a small number of men – who are in real danger, as the system gets clogged up with shallow claims. Police issue violence restraining orders, courts hear family violence allegations, and the Family Court has to deal with cases more carefully as the family violence-risk flag has been raised. All of this slows the system while the protective orders are dropped, and the court does not share the concerns about unacceptable risk.

It is important to understand the different types of family violence, as the term 'family violence' alone does not really indicate what the dangers are, nor the impact on the children. To understand the risk involved, it is important to identify the potency of the violence (the severity and dangerousness), the pattern of how it has been occurring, the primary perpetrator (is there one person, or are both parties reacting to each other?), and the impact it may have on the parenting of the children, or how the child perceives the violence.

Beginning with the basics, anger is an emotion and feeling angry at times is part of the normal human experience. If you have too much anger in your life, seek anger management counselling or psychological therapy as something is not right. It should be an occasional emotion, typically with a clear and justified trigger. While on triggers for both anger and violence, if you ever say it is NOT my fault because they pushed my buttons, then you have failed Family Violence 101. To blame a partner for your reaction is to give your control to them. At worst they have said something provocative and emotional, but you have been triggered, and now you may act on that triggering. It is your responsibility to manage your triggers, not them. If you are the partner on the receiving end of *"you made me do it"* then you are believing a myth and a lie – that it is not your fault. Perhaps they could have been more tactful but everything else is their reaction and choice.

Turning the anger into aggression is where it becomes problematic. The angry feeling now becomes name-calling, or engaging in physical acts like shoving, hitting, pushing. These are family violence episodes. I am still amazed that we are in the 21st century and people are not fully cognisant that this is considered violence. You do not have to be punched or strangled to be a victim of family violence. The more extreme levels of family violence are systematically using threat, intimidation and control to achieve an outcome by using fear and intimidation. At the extreme end, it becomes unwanted intrusion such as stalking, monitoring and related behaviours. I also think it is fascinating that the higher levels of violence are often no longer violence from anger. They are about control and may relate to a deep and enduring rage, not normally triggered by the current emotion of anger.

It is a reality that couples do not separate because they are happy and things are going well. They separate because they are feeling unhappy, and the relationship is not working. Often, towards the end of relationship break-ups, people are miserable, may be suffering depression and feeling tension. With separation, the issues of the instigator and non-instigator's differing emotional journeys come into play. However, the miserable place the relationship is in prior to separation means it may manifest by increased irritability and volatility. A heated argument between two people near the end of a relationship may include name-calling and pushing, and therefore, meets the definition of family violence but is unlikely to be representative of a serious risk when the parties have had a long history of contained behaviour. Once out of the pressure cooker of the unhappy relationship, and especially if they begin to get on with life again, the emotional reactivity rapidly subsides.

Couples who have had no particular history of violence in the marriage, and no coercive controlling behaviours, may become dysregulated towards the end of the relationship and that is a classed as 'separation-instigated violence'. The conflict is often acknowledged, perpetrators often feel embarrassed or ashamed of their actions, and it is usually limited to one or two episodes. It occurs roughly equally for both men and women. The long-term risk is quite low unless a party has decompensated, for example in the case of an affair where they feel excessively wounded.

Some couples have had an unstable relationship where they have had frequent arguments throughout their time together, where they have managed conflicts poorly, which sometimes escalate into physical violence. Therefore, what is happening at the end is not new but an escalation of the existing problems. Typically, these are minor forms of violence such as pushing, shoving, grabbing. Injuries are not common, and the parties are generally not fearful of each other. This is often called 'situational couple violence' or sometimes 'common couple violence'. It is likely the woman throwing a cup of coffee on her partner who was walking out the door, was like this. Such reactions are unacceptable for children as it shows a dysregulated way of dealing with problems but, typically, after separation the problems diminish, although they may need some boundaries in the initial part of the separation.

Situational couple violence becomes riskier and more likely to have longer-term problems when there is a more extended history of aggressive behaviour (to people outside of the relationship), juvenile offending, and often there is evidence of some sort of neuro-cognitive impairment (ADHD, frontal lobe head injuries, etc.). These people dysregulate and the problem may extend not just to couples, but to other people. Essentially, they do not have the handbrake to control their behaviour, and these people are likely, potentially, to spike-up at any time in the future. These people are an ever-present risk as they escalate and cannot regulate.

The most dangerous type of family violence is coercive-controlling violence. Whereas the other types of violence listed are typically occurring for both men and women, the coercive-control violence is predominantly male, and studies find that somewhere between 87 and 97 per cent of the time it is men exercising control over women. Women can be perpetrators, and it is particularly common in lesbian relationships or with women who have a major personality disorder. A key dynamic is that intimidation, coercion and control, and emotional abuse are central dynamics. Some people may be in a relationship but because they were never hit, do not realise it was a coercive-controlling relationship. When violence does occur, it is often more severe and, post-separation, the violence may be more severe than before separation. The violence is likely to be more severe and chronic when the parties have severe personality disorders. This type of violence is harder to predict and does not come from an angry moment but rather a "transgression" (break a rule), or to punish them for not doing something.

I am finding this is one of the most commonly misunderstood forms of violence when discussed in court cases. The most common reason is there may be a behaviour which can be viewed as controlling, for example, cutting off the credit card though the intent to cause fear is not present. The card is cut off because the couple are now separated and finances need to be re-sorted. I agree it was nasty not to tell them it was being cut off while the partner had a trolley full of groceries in the supermarket, but it is not in the league of significant control. It was not done to punish or manipulate the person. Similarly post separation, a party, typically a woman, may reflect they were doing sex for their partner but they did not want to do it, so that was coercive control. Typically, it was done to keep the peace. While there is a control element and unhealthy relationship aspect, it is not centred around fear or control. Being made to have sex with the partner's friend, or a lady who was told if she did not have sex her pet pig would be shot, are situations where coercive control is a significant risk. The fear and intimidation are central.

When people leave seriously coercive relationships, they will need assistance to leave safely, and it is important to note that often the problems can go for years. It may extend into stalking. For example, the case I had where a couple were living in the country, and the father had threatened to shoot the mother's pet pig if she did not comply with his sexual request. She did not comply, so he shot the pig. If that was not bad enough, three years post-separation when they were selling the house, as she went to do a final clean of the property, he had dug up the pig's skull and left it on the kitchen table for her.

Stalking is perhaps one of the most disturbing forms of violence which can occur because people remain constantly scared. In this day and age, stalking can involve electronic means, tracking devices, as well as traditional following and observing. It can include cutting off friends, visiting workplaces to shame the victim, and so forth. However, it is important to differentiate the context as it is not the behaviour alone which determines an act to be stalking. At the start of the relationship, somebody ringing you 20 times a day to see how you are and to express their love, might be seen as a sign of love and devotion, although this should also be seen as a warning sign. In the first week after separation, 20 phone calls in a day mostly reflects a desperate attempt to try to reconnect by a grieving non-initiator. However, if this is occurring 12 months' later, especially after a warning to cease sending messages, it is likely to be an indicator of a significant problem and be stalking. Context and potency of a behaviour are critical.

Situations can also get complicated. A parent is suspicious their partner may be having an affair. They put a tracking device in a car for a week and catch the partner out by going to the location and finding them with the other person – the partner was lying as to their actual location (they were saying they were 60km away on a mine site). That act alone may or may not be legal (tracking the car can be illegal), and the person is being monitored without their knowledge or consent. The big question is, is it justified because they are having an affair (realistic justification), or not appropriate because it was without their knowledge and consent? This is the grey end of stalking. If they have been separated for a year and an active tracking device is found in the car, it is clearly stalking and not justifiable.

Children seeing their parents having a disagreement and successfully resolving it are learning an important life skill. Children seeing their parents having arguments and losing it emotionally, are going to learn poor ways of modelling behaviour. However, children being fearful that their parent is being hurt, or they may be hurt, are likely to experience significant levels of trauma. I would note that parents who are coercively controlling or have a history of physical harm to adults have an increased risk of physically and mentally harming children.

The victim of significant family violence frequently experiences depression and may experience post-traumatic stress disorder. Therefore, they will have difficulty regulating their emotions and being emotionally present for the child. The sad reality is people who have been victims of significant family violence may be impaired in their capacity to parent. I note that parents will quickly get help for children but may be slower to get their own intervention. If you were a victim and have depression and PTSD, get help. There is a type of trauma therapy called EMDR (Eye Movement Desensitisation and Reprocessing) which is an excellent tool for quickly lowering trauma memories for PTSD.

The coercive-controlling parent in the relationship may well have been determined to destroy the child's self-esteem in the relationship so as to control the child. After separation the game changes and the children are now the prize to hurt the other parent. Therefore, post-separation, the coercive controller may try to manipulate the child to their own ends. They give the child special treatment and reward compliance. In another variant, a child may align with the coercive controller for safety reasons (align with the strong not the weak). Therefore, the implications and impacts of family violence are complex and multi-faceted. Hearing the child report their relationship with the coercive parent is good does not always mean it is healthy.

Parents who dysregulate in an argument may be able to learn anger management and regulation strategies. People with neuro-cognitive issues may be able to be managed by medication and therapy strategies. However, for those who are high on coercive control, especially if they have personality disorders, going to therapy may actually make them better able to manipulate people by speaking the language of recovery (when they have not actually changed) and sounding repentant, while maintaining their controlling behaviour. Often group treatments are more successful than individual therapy in breaking down the dynamics of family violence.

Key points:

- Anger is an emotion; aggression is a behaviour. It is appropriate to be angry at times, but aggression needs to be channelled into appropriate strategies.

- All family violence should be taken seriously and, ideally, properly assessed to determine risk.

- There are three common types of family violence, which include separation-induced, situational couple violence, and coercive-controlling violence. Coercive-controlling violence is by far the most sinister and has the greatest risks attached to it.

- When people leave seriously coercive relationships, they will need assistance to exit safely. The greater the risk the more help required to leave.

- There are some legal professionals who, in my opinion, are over-using family violence claims as a trump card when, in fact, there is no particular risk to the children. While this may win a case for the client, it does a disservice to those women who are subject to the more sinister forms of violence.

Parenting Styles

When parenting after separation is looked at in broad terms, the most helpful model for children's long-term wellbeing is what is called "co-parenting". Using the analogy of two lines, co-parenting sees two lines on top of each other going in the same direction. In the model, the lines are hand-drawn such that at times there are small gaps, but generally it looks like one line drawn toward a common destination.

Co-parenting is where the two parents may live in separate houses but they work co-operatively for the wellbeing of the children. Just like when they were in the marriage relationship the parents are still able to talk about what is best for the children, both on a major level and on a day-to-day basis. Co-parenting means the parents have very similar styles of discipline, objectives for the children and, most importantly, have the capacity to co-operate.

Co-parenting requires communication and some level of respect. It does not require parents to have identical beliefs or systems because even when two parents are living together, they do not necessarily function in this way. Children can tolerate a fair degree of ambiguity between parents, and as long as the general methods are similar, then children do well. What child does not try asking mum, and then dad, for something because they hope one will weaken?

If raising children is seen as a business where there is a general plan about what both parents believe is a successful outcome, and they structure the process to enable it to happen, then co-parenting is likely. This is what I would call psychological shared care, as opposed to the legal definition (working together versus having blocks of shared time). You do not need to like someone to co-parent. What you need to be able to co-parent is to love your children more than you hate your ex-partner!

This is why the 2006 legislation in Australia was not very effective – ordering parents to legally share the time does not mean co-parenting has taken place. The court can only order time, it cannot order people to be business partners who respect each other as parents. It is also important to note the court cannot order people to have similar parenting styles.

The next level down from co-parenting is what is called "parallel parenting". Using the same analogy, the two lines have distance between them but are pointing roughly in the same direction. Here the parents are unable to work jointly, but both are generally moving in the same direction. During their time with the children, they do their own thing, but they are both doing it in a similar fashion. These couples are likely to have had similar beliefs and values prior to separation so they continue to go on doing what they have always done.

For many couples, parallel parenting is the best model that can be achieved. This is because it does not require a joint relationship, but the parents are psychologically mature enough to do what is best for the children. At a psychological level, when this style is at its best and functions well, it is second-rate shared care – the children still have a sense of security, and the parents are able to provide stable and predictable worlds. At its worst, it is divided care because the children know that there are boundaries between the two worlds. The children are less likely to have mum and dad together at their teacher-parent meetings (they come at different times) and are less likely to have both of their parents attend a sports day. Each parent takes the children to the same sporting event during "their time", and at the grand final both parents will be there but on opposite sides of the oval.

The closer the two parallel lines, the nearer the situation will be to shared care, and therefore better for the children. By closer I mean parents who can talk directly, even if only superficially, will model better attitudes, rather than parents who only communicate by email or message books. However, this is still closer than parents who do not talk at all and simply do their own thing. Parallel parenting attempts to achieve an illusion of shared care, as this is better for children than seeing their parents at odds with each other.

In the parallel parenting model, there may be a dominant line. This may always have been the case, or it may have emerged post-separation. The other parent has a dilemma – to follow that line or carve their own direction. For the sake of the children, a healthy parent will be psychologically mature enough to compromise so that they move in the same direction as the other parent, even if they do not fully agree with that course of action.

My observation of parenting styles suggests there are two other common parenting styles. One is the style I have recently termed "remote-control parenting". This occurs where a parent, particularly a mother, has a very high expectation of what should occur and is quite controlling within the parental relationship.

As described in earlier sections, it is quite common that mothers in particular, like to cocoon the child in a protective bubble. One of our jokes about my wife's parenting of our children when they were babies, relates to the 'mat time' rug. The children used to have a mat they would lie on during mat time. Even the dog knew to walk around the mat rather than walk on it! From a hygiene point of view, my wife's actions were extremely appropriate; however, I do not think I would have had the tenacity to do it as pedantically as she did. She was the dominant line and I followed so that the children had consistency.

When parents separate, a problem arises when the dominant parent tries to dictate to the other parent how to do things to the same level. These are cases where one party dictates where the line is to be drawn, and they will not allow for any other possibility. I was involved in a case where the mother wrote a whole page in the communication book detailing, among other things, how to wipe the child's bottom properly and, in a list of foods, she specified every brand of food to be given (not just the type). The father would receive a barrage of criticism if he varied from her extremely high and rigid standards. It is important to note I am not talking about an incompetent father who cannot manage tasks, but cases in which the parents are high functioning (in this case the father was an accountant who had previously raised a child successfully). At the end of the day, children will grow up perfectly fine if some meals are a takeaway bought chicken and not an organic chicken breast!

It is normal for the primary parent, especially the mother, to be protective and to want consistency. I think it is a good thing for the child. However, there is a point where the situation goes from sharing the child's routines and practices to controlling the activities of the other parent. It can be a problem in the relationship while a couple is together – one parent will feel marginalised in their parenting activities. However, after separation (and this is commonly a factor leading to the separation – the partner needing to free themselves from the control) the dominant parent still wants to have the control. In these situations, the partner is no longer present but the other still wants to control from a distance. The remote-control parent will experience anxiety. It is going to cause tremendous problems – each time the child leaves, the controlling parent will feel anxiety, fear and panic. To deal with their anxiety, they try to regain control by giving further instructions. Their ex-partner is going to feel highly resentful and the dynamics in these circumstances are extremely difficult.

During one Family Court trial, the judge started by saying to the father words to the effect that, *What you do during your time is entirely up to you, as long as it is not illegal, immoral or dangerous*, and then turned to the other parent and said to her, *What the father does during his time is none of your business and you have to let it go*. This may seem like a bitter pill to swallow, however, this is the practical reality after separation, and parents need to learn to let go. It is also classic parallel parenting given from the bench. Unfortunately, it is not in the children's best interests.

Having said that, it is important that there is some compromise in parallel parenting. The judge's statement is certainly true in that parents do have a right to enjoy their time with their children unhindered by the other parent. However, the rights of the parents do not replace the psychological needs of the child. The child does need similar routines. In other words, you may not like to eat at 5.30pm but if that is when the child eats most of their dinners, then it is better to stick to something close to that time, rather than eat whenever you think it is appropriate resulting in the child having two routines.

The remote-control pattern of parenting is going to be extremely destructive to both parents and to the children in the longer term. It can never be shared care at a psychological level because one party is essentially dictating the rules. Children do need what both parents can offer. The child who is most balanced has learned different things from mum and dad. As stated earlier, a father is likely to allow a child a greater degree of exploration in the world (and as a result there may be a few extra falls requiring Band-Aids). Children need to explore the world and master their bodies, and the remote-control parent will almost always inhibit such actions.

The most important implication for a controlling parent is that the child will eventually want to break free if that parent does not relax and let go first. Therefore, during the child's teenage years, the controlling parent may find that the child packs up and moves in with the other parent. If the control has been too tight, they may not come back.

A fourth type of parenting is what I call "crossover" parenting. Here the two parents have very different styles or beliefs. The lines run in different directions. For example, I recently saw a case where the mother did not believe the four-year-old daughter should have make-up or painted nails, but the father allowed it anyway because *the little girl likes it and no one's going to take it away from her because it's her right.* They could not agree on which dance class the child should go to, so the poor little girl had two different dance classes on alternate Saturdays. In this particular case the father argued for shared care, wanting the child on a 50 per cent basis. Psychologically, this would have been a disaster because their parenting styles were mutually exclusive; the father had poor boundaries and gave in to the child, the mother was firm and, in my opinion, appropriate. (The mother's nail polish ban was appropriate in that the child's kindergarten did not allow children to wear nail polish.) Such differences in parenting styles can only lead to disaster.

All parents have some minor issues which cross over. These are usually compromised or resolved. What I am talking about here is where the primary styles or beliefs are fundamentally different. Crossover parenting is almost impossible to deal with on a shared-care basis. If parents have opposing beliefs and styles, and they cannot put the beliefs to one side, then the child will be in constant confusion. For example, in one case, one parent believed in God and would teach the child to pray, while the other parent would mock prayer and teach the child that there was no God. In another case, the mother enrolled the child in soccer and the father would spend his time disparaging the game and complaining the child should play Australian Rules.

A related set of problems comes from differing discipline styles. For example, one parent believes in time-out as a consequence, while the other parent believes a child should not be told off or punished and should be reasoned with. Here, the dynamics produce a good parent and a mean parent in the eyes of the child even though both parents are using acceptable parenting styles. In these cases, confusion and tension will be the constant companion in the child's life. This is divided care at its worst.

This review of parenting styles in separation clearly shows that the positive parent, who has the best interests of the child at heart, should strive for co-parenting. This is the only pathway to real shared care. If you cannot achieve co-parenting, then parallel parenting is the next best option and, depending on how parallel you become, you may either provide children with the illusion of shared care or you simply divide their life. Remote control or crossover parenting styles are not just difficult for establishing shared care but are psychologically destructive to children in both the short and long term.

Key points

- Co-parenting is where the two parents live in separate houses but they work co-operatively for the wellbeing of the children. The parents are able to communicate about what is best for the children, both for their future and on a day-to-day basis.

- If raising children is seen as a business where there is a general plan about what both parents believe is a successful outcome, and they structure the life to enable it to happen, then children will benefit.

- You do not need to like someone to co-parent. What you need in order to co-parent is to love your children more than you hate your ex-partner!

- The next level down from co-parenting is what is called "parallel parenting". Here the parents are unable to work directly together but both are generally moving in the same direction. During their time with the children, they do their own thing, but they are both doing it in a similar fashion. These couples are likely to have had similar beliefs and values prior to separation, so they continue to go on doing what they have always done.

- At a psychological level, even if parallel parenting is functioning well, it is second-rate shared care. Nevertheless, the children will still have a sense of security and the parents are able to provide stable and predictable worlds.

- Remote-control parenting arises when a dominant parent tries to dictate to the other parent how to do things during their own time. The child who is most balanced will safely learn different things from both mum and dad, rather than having to fit into a single pattern of parenting.

- Crossover parenting is where the parents have very different styles or beliefs which are incompatible. This is damaging to the child and conflicting for the parents. Children should not be in shared care if the parenting styles are that incompatible.

- If parents cannot co-parent, then parallel parenting is the next best option and, depending on how parallel a parent becomes, they may either provide children with the illusion of shared care or are simply dividing the child's life. Remote control or crossover parenting styles are not just difficult for establishing shared care but are psychologically destructive to children in both the short and long term.

The United Front

Just as there are various behaviours that create negative outcomes for children, there are certain behaviour patterns that create positive outcomes. While you have no control over how your partner acts, you can control yourself. You have the power to promote the wellbeing of your children through your actions. As stated earlier, there is no such thing as neutral behaviour. You choose whether to build them up or damage them.

The parents who are going to achieve the best outcomes for the children in a separation situation need to work with a united front. This means everything from telling the children in advance about the separation, sharing similar explanations of what is going on, through to dealing with conflict in a united manner.

Children wanting to play off their parents is a problem which will emerge. Let's face reality – children play off parents in the same house. I remember asking my mum if I could go camping and she said I could go if dad let me. When I saw dad, I would say that mum had said I could! Once parents separate, in the emotional turmoil of separation, guilt is a common emotion which makes them more vulnerable to being playoff by the children. They feel guilty for what they are putting the children through and often will want to buy their children's affections. Children quickly sense this and will play on it. This can occur with little things such as asking one parent to buy something and then the other parent feeling they have to compensate. I have been involved in cases where children have two sets of absolutely everything from the latest PlayStation equipment to bicycles and Barbie dolls. This results in children being over-indulged.

At a more significant level, there is a need for a united front with older children. A very common scenario is one in which a teenager has a fight with one parent, and then rings the other parent and says, *"I want to come and live with you."* The healthy parent says, *"Well, we'll sort that out together as parents and let you know what the outcome is, but we will talk you through your current situation."* The unhealthy parent sneaks around to the back door in the middle of the night, loads the child into the car and takes off. In the short-term it may have taken the child out of a difficult situation; in the longer term it has totally undermined both parents' authority base because the child now has no respect for one parent and can manipulate the other. It will only be a matter of time before this child will have lost respect for both parents.

The united front also means observing similar time frames and similar discipline styles. Routines should be as similar as possible, as should consequences for actions. There is no one way to parent children, but using similar styles is important. I am a qualified and experienced child psychologist, but my wife had the majority of parenting time because she worked part-time and I worked full time. She had primary day-to-day care of the children. Therefore, while I may not have fully agreed with some of her parenting approaches, I would go with it to avoid confusion with the children. I may have had a better way or different way, but it was healthier for the children to only have the one way.

With respect to time frames, it is important for children to have structure and routine. If one parent lets a child stay up late, and the other parent enforces a strict bedtime, children may enjoy the time with the more liberal parent. However, there will be consequences in terms of the children's learning and education, moodiness and so on, which will take its toll. It is important for children, particularly younger children, to have regular routines. I would go so far as to say that regular routines are one of the most important structures for mentally health children. If a child has special needs such as autism, ADHD or a disability, predictable and structured routines are even more important.

Key points

- Children in separated families have a greater opportunity to play off their parents than children in intact families. The only cure is communication and co-operation.

- In the emotional turmoil of separation, guilt is a common emotion. Parents feel guilty for what they are putting the children through and often will want to buy their children's affections. Parents must not overcompensate by excessively buying things for their children.

- There is no one way to parent children, but using similar styles is important. A united front means observing similar time frames and similar discipline styles. Routines should be kept as similar as possible, as should consequences for actions.

Neuro-atypical, ADHD and Separation

We live in a time where the diagnosis of neuro-atypical children (and adults) is rapidly escalating. Twenty years ago, recognising and diagnosing attention deficit hyperactivity disorder (ADHD) took-off. In the past 10 years there has been a rapid expansion in the diagnosis of autistic spectrum disorder (ASD). With this condition, there are additional variants, such as pathological demand avoidance (PDA), oppositional defiance disorder (ODD), sensory processing disorders, and related neuro-atypical conditions. This is not the place to debate why there is an increase in diagnoses. Essentially, more children are being identified earlier, and adults who were never diagnosed are now seeking to apply labels to themselves to help them understand why they are functioning the way they have been through their life.

There are several distinct advantages to having a label. The first advantage is that it allows professionals to talk to each other about the problems a condition may present and to target treatment around the type of condition. Furthermore, labels often allow for funding. There are different government funds available for different types of diagnosed conditions in both children and adults. Sometimes I wonder if children are getting pushed across the line for a diagnosis to get funding. In some cases, this may be true, but in many cases the diagnosis is warranted and justified. Regardless, the diagnosis is made and the court and workers in the area have to make considerations for the child given they have additional issues to address within the separation process.

There are also downsides to diagnostic labelling. The first point I would like to stress with diagnosis is that there is not a standard treatment based on diagnosis. I run a boutique clinic which involves treating various brain-based conditions using neurofeedback. Neurofeedback looks at the EEG of the brain and uses training sessions to improve performance in the problem area, be it attention, learning difficulties, anxiety or dysregulation. A good assessment is necessary to enable successful treatment. However, the treatment is based on the unique individual, not the diagnosis. What I am saying is everybody with a condition is unique. A 21-year-old who I know well was studying chemistry at university and was on the vice-chancellor's list but, in a conversation, talks at you rather than reciprocally, and has a crow decomposing in the back garden. She is diagnosed with high-functioning ASD. A friend's child of similar age rocks in the corner building playdough models of dinosaurs. He is also diagnosed with ASD. Both manifest differently. Just saying one is level one and other is level three tells us almost nothing about what they are like or what they can do.

This means that, when considering arrangements for children with certain conditions, the label alone will not determine 'time-with' arrangements. However, there is a greater level of consideration to making those arrangements work. The first aspect is that in almost any behavioural condition, the psychological advice is routine and structure. Generally-speaking, the more predictable the routine, the better children with ASD or ADHD can function in the home. Therefore, often the parent with the most routine is going to provide the best environment. Noting that a number of these conditions run in the family, there may be a parent who is also ASD or ADHD, and they may not be able to put in place the structure or, alternatively, may have learned to cope by being hyper-structured. The simple implication is the more similar both parents are in their structure, the greater the options for the children.

The second aspect is dealing with different behavioural issues. Somebody once said that ASD diagnoses do not travel alone but have friends and those friends include anxiety, OCD, learning difficulties and oppositional defiance. Consequently, there is a primary condition with additional factors which need to be managed. Anxiety is a common problem. Anxious children, again, need structure but may also be better handled by one of the parents.

Sometimes, equal arrangements will work, at other times it is important to consider whether longer periods of time will be better. In a normal situation with younger children, attachment is a priority so short, frequent visits are recommended. However, children with special needs sometimes have to prioritise the routine and structure over attachment. It may be better if the visits are longer and less frequent for the children to cope.

One of the models I use to explain to parents with autistic spectrum disordered (ASD) children is the bucket model. As a child goes through the day, their bucket fills up with emotion. Neurotypical children have ways of emptying the bucket throughout the day, while ASD children typically keep filling the bucket. When they get home from their day, either the parent helps calm them or they then engage in quiet-time behaviours, including computer games or alone time to lower the level of their bucket. Otherwise, they become dysregulated. Sometimes, if parents have diverse levels of attachment, the primary parent will cop a lot more behavioural difficulties because the child feels safe to dysregulate. When they see the less attached parent, their behaviour may be good and I often see claims that, "The child is good with me, therefore, there must be a problem at the other house." The reality is often more the function of how the child is regulating themselves. At the non-primary house, they are still filling the bucket, not emptying it.

A related issue is that children with ASD manifest in different ways at different ages. A reasonable proportion of children who develop ASD start normally and then regress suddenly around two years old. I was involved in a case where the father was trying to argue that the mother must be abusing the child because the child was regressing and losing language. He had videos to show the child's previously talkative nature, compared to their current functioning. I immediately advised the father that the child was showing signs of autism and the child was later diagnosed as such.

Where children have pathological demand avoidance (PAS) and oppositional defiance disorder (ODD), parenting can be extremely hard. School refusal, behavioural problems, parental visit refusal and so forth are very taxing. The more the parents are in court, the less flexibility there is to deal with situations. These are complex dynamics which need flexibility. The problems need good communication, and flexibility with the ex-partner is the absolute key. When parents cannot work together, one parent may need to be given the parental authority to engage help speedily if the parties are arguing too much against each other.

While not all gender-diverse people have ASD, a higher-than-expected proportion do. It makes perfect sense in that they are trying to make sense of their identity and do not feel they fit in the neurotypical world. Therefore, gender identity may become a concern. However, there are children who are not ASD who also have gender-diverse interests and yearning. Either way, it is important for parents to remember there are two broad aspects to identity formation in this age group. One is that the teenage years are where gender identity emerges, and the second aspect is that people experiment with different beliefs to find beliefs that fit them. Sometimes, their beliefs grow and become part of their long-term identity, but many young people will drop these beliefs and identity after trying it for a while and experiment with other beliefs and identities.

There is no way of knowing what the long-term outcome will be. For example, those who are older will remember seeing punks, goths and other identities in the 14 to 25-year-old age group but we now rarely see them as they get older. Therefore, it is critically important not to lock the child into a particular position around their gender identity but to be supportive of them through this experience. If you argue against the child, they may try harder to rebel and you have actually reinforced their beliefs (the Romeo and Juliette effect). On the other hand, if you over-validate their gender issues, you may push them toward something they are not ready for – such as hormone treatment and surgery – and should they evolve into different beliefs it will be harder to change back.

Where two parents disagree, it will become even harder for the child and they typically side with the most supportive parent. All families have different beliefs and expectations, but it is so much easier for the young person if the main players are all on the same page.

The central point is loving your child, being there for them, and helping them see the situation through mature eyes and allowing them an informed approach. Ultimately, they have to live their lives and you have no control. What you do not want is to push them away from you. It can be very hard for a parent to see a child push against their key values. However, it is also a hard and lonely place for the young person to go against everything they have been taught and experienced.

Key Points

- All children are unique, and diagnosis does not determine the outcome for the child. It simply helps explain some aspects of who they are and why they do what they do.

- Autism and ADHD do not rule out the possibility of shared care or equal shared care. However, they do require a more nuanced understanding of what will impact the child.

- Neuro-atypical children need the most school time with the parent who can provide the best routine and structure and can help empty the bucket of stress they accumulate each day.

- Gender diversity is a difficult issue for many parents. Your child needs to feel loved and valued though this process. Disagreeing with the former partner may serve to cause the child to take sides.

Some Practical Parenting Points

One of the biggest tests of the maturity of the parent is their ability to be able to maintain for their children a healthy psychological picture of their ex-partner. The fact a person is an ex-partner means the parent is likely to resent, and perhaps hate, that person. If they want their children to cope well, they need to keep those feelings shielded from their children and, more importantly, create some sort of positive image. Ideally, a parent should work through their feelings until they form a genuine positive view of the ex-partner, but if they are unable to do that, then the next best compromise is to create a positive illusion for the children.

A positive illusion occurs when a parent asks if the child has had a good time, encourages them to go on visits, and takes an interest in the sorts of things the children have been doing. It is important it is not done as an inquisition to find fault, and that the children are allowed to talk about it in their own time. If a parent disagrees with an action, it is important not to totally knock the situation. If the parent shows strong negative reactions to the things that have been occurring, then the children learn to be secretive, tell the parent what they think the parent wants to hear, and take sides.

Having pictures of the other parent in the house or child's bedroom, giving access to photo albums of when the parents were together, and allowing the child to bring things from the other parent into the home are beneficial strategies in modelling support.

A healthy parent points out there may be different rules and different ways of doing things in their house. Therefore, you do not have to agree with everything the ex-partner does. The approach is that you are "different" and have "different rules", not that you are "right" and the other parent is "wrong". The key is not to make it a major issue, at least not directly with the children, but it may be something to discuss with the partner through your communication process.

As people go through the separation process, re-partnering becomes a significant issue. For the majority of children there is a strong desire for their parents to reunite. The wish for their parents to get back together is something that they hold for many years. One study found 50 per cent of children were still fantasising about their parents being together again 10 years after the separation. A new partner is a threat to this wish or desire. Therefore, new partners often feel the brunt of the children's psychological issues. The children may attempt to stop the partner from forming a relationship with their parent by being difficult, mean or angry. It is important not to re-partner too quickly or you may have another failed relationship. (My book *How to Find Love and Not a Psycho* is a good read for parents choosing a new partner.)

A child may also be very needy and may wish for a new partner to come into their lives. For example, in a Family Court case I saw a five-year-old girl in my office for one hour, and then on a home visit to her mother's house she said to me, "*You should marry my mummy, I need a new daddy*". What this little girl was saying in clear terms was she was very needy as a result of the break-up of her parents, and she was desperate to take anybody to try to make her life whole again. Therefore, a new partner may be either quickly accepted or may be the product of anger and bitterness over a long period of time.

My simple rule of thumb is that if you have come out of a major long-term relationship it will probably take three more relationships before you will be psychologically in a position to deal effectively with a new long-term partner. Therefore, if the first two dating experiences are not going to last, it is critical these people are not introduced into the lives of your children, or at least not significantly. I am amazed at how many people will have a new partner living in the home within months of their first meeting. This complicates the lives of children. While I understand that parents are desperate and needy too, it is not in the children's best interests. Therefore, the healthy parent will be careful not to introduce new partners too quickly, and they are sensitive to their children's needs (either to try to fill a hole, or to see their parents back together again).

Some parents have the mistaken view the new partner will create a new family for the child and the old partner will not be necessary. A new partner may fill a very important role in the family and provide a good role model. However, the new partner is not biologically connected to the child. As noted earlier, the child is a product of both parents, which has implications at deep emotional levels. Hopefully, the new partner provides an excellent additional role model. That is, they add something else, not replace something.

The use of "mum" and "dad" are common grounds for arguments. If you re-partner it is important to let the children decide what and when to call the new partner. Younger children are more inclined to want to call them mum or dad sooner. It also becomes common when other children are in the house using the names. The other parent sometimes takes issue with someone else being called mum or dad. In my opinion it does not matter if the child has two mums and two dads. What matters is whether they know who their biological mum and dad are. It can be helpful to use variations on names such as mummy and mimmi, dad and daddy.

The discipline role of the new partner is complicated. If they parent equally from the start the children will hate them. If they do not discipline, the children will not respect them. My rule of thumb is that the amount of parenting they take on is equal to the percentage they have been in the child's life. A new partner has been around for two years. One child is four years old, the other is 10 years old. Two years in the life of a four-year-old is 50 per cent and two years in the life of the 10-year-old is 20 per cent. The new partner should be doing about 50 per cent of what the biological parent does for the first child but only 20 per cent for the older child.

At a basic level, separation means change. Parents once lived together in one house. In the most stable situation, one parent stays in the family home while the other parent buys a house in the same area. The children remain in the same school, keep the same friends and have the security of staying in the same house. As described earlier, children develop a sense of attachment not just to people but also to their environment and networks. They also have a whole set of social and emotional support through their community networks.

When separation occurs, people move. They may move far away, taking their children out of their school and social network. This may be a practical reality. A couple living together can afford to live in a better suburb. Post-separation, one or both parents may have to move to a cheaper suburb, the family home may have to be sold, a parent may have temporary rental accommodation prior to property settlement, and so forth.

However, for the children's sake, it is better for the children if parents either don't move, or don't move very far away.

I have had several cases where the desire to stay in the family home has been the toughest aspect of the court battle. The "winning" parent keeps the house. Similarly, I have had cases where parents have borrowed excessively to keep the family home because the teenage child did not want to move. The house should not be a prize, and children should not be dictating the family's future. The acid test is to ask yourself: If you were not in the middle of a separation, would you take this course of action? The child who does not want you to sell the family home is welcome to their view, but would you normally base your decision entirely on their wants?

The positive parent will make sure the emotional needs of both themselves and their children are adequately addressed. In my opinion, the quicker parents can resolve their own emotions, particularly if depression and anger are present, the better it will be for the wellbeing and adjustment of the children. Therefore, it is important for parents to recognise that if they suffer from these conditions, they should seek both psychological and medical/psychiatric assistance as quickly as possible. Fortunately, in Australia the stigma associated with therapy and counselling is diminishing. Therefore, more people are seeking help, and help is more readily available.

One caution to note is that therapy is based around the client. Therefore, the therapist is primarily going to take responsibility for the person who walks through the door. Therefore, if you seek counselling, the counsellor will specifically address your wellbeing. It takes a very experienced and competent counsellor to help you to understand not just your own wellbeing, but also the implications for your children. To assist the counsellor, it is important you take responsibility for putting on the agenda for your discussions the issues associated with decisions affecting children. In this society, the rate of separation is increasing as people become more individually focused. This very issue is a problem that can occur with therapy. Therefore, it is important to ensure your children's needs are high on the agenda.

The old-fashioned value where the parent makes sacrifices for the children is now one which is sometimes labelled as co-dependent or is seen as a block to self-actualisation. In my opinion, this is somewhat sad as it is clouding the fact that when parents have children, they also take on a responsibility and an obligation. It is necessary for a parent to sacrifice some of their short-term happiness for the wellbeing of the children. It is an old-fashioned value that should be complemented. It is particularly so in a case of separation, where everyone may be suffering, that children need to be a priority. I would qualify my comments to say that parents who live through their children are as unhealthy as parents who live for themselves. It is balance that is needed.

Key points

- The maturer parent is to be able to maintain a healthy psychological picture of their ex-partner for their children. Talking nicely about the ex-partner, retaining pictures of them in the house, and being supportive toward them are important factors for the children.

- A positive illusion of the other parent can be created when a parent encourages the child to go on a visit, asks if the child has had a good time on the visit, and takes an interest in the sorts of things the child has been doing with the other parent.

- The healthy parent will be careful not to introduce new partners into the lives of the children too quickly and remain sensitive to their children's needs.

- A new partner may fill a very important role in the family and provide a good role model. However, the new partner is not biologically connected to the child. Do not assume a new partner can fill all the psychological needs of the child.

- Children can easily cope with having two mums and two dads as long as they know who their biological parent is.

- The discipline role of the new partner is complicated. My rule of thumb is the amount of parenting they take on is equal to the percentage they have been in the child's life.

- "Sameness" is important for a child's adjustment. The more you can keep the routines and environment the same, the better the child adjusts.

- The positive parent will make sure their own and their children's emotional are adequately addressed. The more quickly parents can resolve their own emotions, particularly if depression and anger are present, the better it will be for the wellbeing and adjustment of the children.

- A therapist is primarily going to take responsibility for the person who walks through the door. When a parent seeks counselling, the counsellor will specifically address their client's wellbeing. It takes a very experienced and competent counsellor to help the parent understand not just their own wellbeing but also any implications for the children.

- Society often labels the parent who makes sacrifices for the children as co-dependent. In my opinion this is clouding the fact that when parents have children they also take on a responsibility and an obligation. It is necessary for a parent to sacrifice some of their short-term happiness, especially during a separation, for the wellbeing of the children.

4

Reaching Agreement

Your son and daughter will only ever have one first day at school, one marriage reception, and one graduation ceremony. They may get critically ill and be in hospital. They may have a serious car accident. In other words, life happens. Sooner or later, you need to get it sorted out with your ex-partner so you can both be there when your child really needs you. I can't imagine what it must have felt like to be the parents of a 10-year-old boy critically ill in the children's hospital and given a 40 per cent chance of being alive in 12 months, and then having to go to court to determine which parent would have him on release from hospital care! True story. Parents need to work these things out and not have turf wars when the children need them.

During the process of separation, one of the most important variables for the wellbeing of the child is your ability to provide a consistent environment in a time of rapid change. To do this you need to be able to negotiate many issues, large and small, with your ex-partner so that the child has as much as possible of the same world in two houses. Unfortunately, there is a fundamental problem associated with achieving this goal. The very person with whom you must co-operate is the same person you were unable to have a successful ongoing relationship with. You have broken up because you cannot agree on important life events.

Typically, there is a fundamental difference of belief that leads people to separate in the first place. Trying to override this difference in an attempt to make the parenting relationship work becomes too difficult for some people. They must deal with their issues within the context of an emotional separation, and in the absence of their former commitment. However, the ability to deal with parenting issues is the very factor which will have the most benefit for the children. The process of reaching agreement to a level that allows for co-parenting is something that even psychologically healthy, well-adjusted, committed people struggle to do. Add to this the emotions described in the earlier chapters and the situation is ripe for warfare, not agreement.

Ultimately, there are three broad strategic approaches to resolving the differing perspectives on the needs of the children. The first is to find a way of reaching agreement together. This is the preferred option. It may be hard, but if you both have input into the outcome, it has the greatest chance of success.

The second is to find solutions through mediation. Mediation provides the opportunity to discuss issues in the presence of a third party. This person has the role of keeping you on track and preventing emotions from getting out of hand while you reach agreement. A related approach in family law has been developed called "collaborative law". It involves the parents, with specially trained lawyers, seeking solutions for the issues to do with children and property by direct negotiation but without the prospect of litigation (collaborative lawyers will not go to court). I see collaborative law as a type of mediation, but the parties do it with lawyers, not a mediator.

The third strategy is to go to court and have an independent arbitrator impose a solution upon you. Court is the most interesting and most volatile strategy to add into the already complicated set of issues. However, there is a very important place for the legal process, and at times it is necessary to involve lawyers in your dispute. The point I would like to stress is there can be an advantage in going to court to have a person impose a solution when neither side can agree or act rationally. The downside is the process tends to escalate the differences already present and takes the decision-making out of the hands of the parents – those who are the most important people in the children's lives. It has the potential to cost large amounts of money which most parents cannot afford. To put it another way, the money spent on barristers at a trial can be more than the entire school fees for two children in a top-tier private school for their entire education.

To understand what approach you may need, it is important to understand there is a gradual process to building a relationship. See the diagram for a visual representation of this process. You start as acquaintances where there is no emotional connection, just someone you say "hi" to or smile at in passing. You then work on a "business" level where you each do things for the other for practical returns. Here, business is used in a very general way. Then you become intimately associated and share an emotional connection as a friend, and this then extends to being lovers. As you go along this process, the emotions become increasingly strong.

The Relationship Process

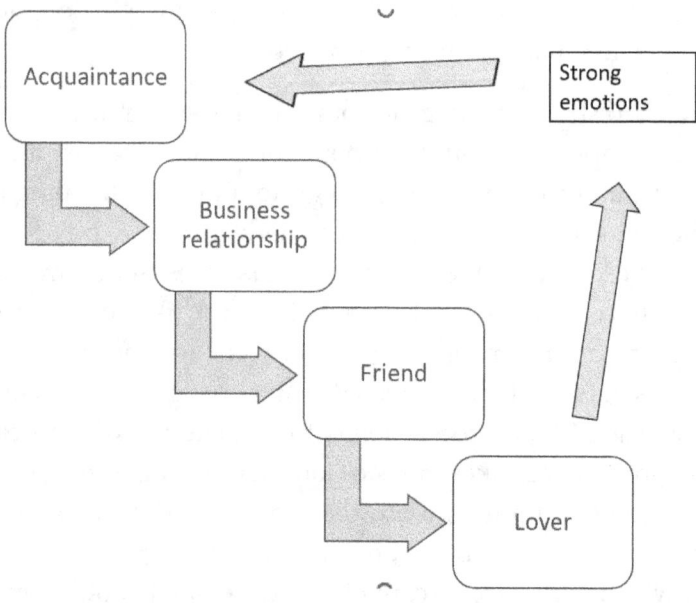

When a couple breaks up, there are negative emotions associated with the break-up which help the couple to disconnect. These feelings include a lack of trust, anger and betrayal. The idea of "let's be friends" is quaint but not psychologically practical. You have to go back through the cycle. After the anger, the arrangement must become that of acquaintances (being civil with each other), then business partners before becoming friends again (and please do not let it go back to intimate!). If one of you has come around so you have some friendship, then negotiating is possible. If you are at the business partner level, mediation makes sense if you cannot negotiate. If you are still in the angry disconnection phase, then arbitration may be necessary.

In the area of stress research, it has been established that life events have a cumulative impact. A typical Life Events Inventory rates the death of a partner as 100 points of stress. A major life event like separation and divorce is approximately 70 points. Various other factors, including moving house, changed financial position, changing jobs or a changing relationship with children, add different levels of points. These various points of stress quickly add up. The more points of stress, the larger the psychological and physical impact on a person's wellbeing. High points increase the risk of major illnesses (such as breast cancer, heart disease and other health problems) and also lower immune system efficacy so as to increase the number of many minor ailments (such as colds and flu). Very high stress is also associated with increased risks of a variety of mental health problems, including depression. Therefore, the separation process has many cumulative sources of stress which will impact upon a person's life in a variety of ways.

Seeking a legal solution elevates an already high stress point tally even further. Court processes have a stress level similar to separation and divorce. However, associated with the court process is a high probability there will be financial pressures, time pressures and various other indirect impacts. Therefore, unless there is an overriding reason to have a legal solution, it is best not to add this stress to your already overstressed world. In cases where parents abscond with children, or where there is domestic violence or other serious allegations, you may be left with no choice but to use a legal process to settle the issue. The point I would like you to consider is that the legal process does not simplify but can complicate reaching agreement.

When a separating couple use lawyers to settle their parenting disputes, they often open Pandora's box. I believe legal processes are important to ensure people maintain their rights and all aspects of a situation are adequately addressed. The problem arises because there is an adversarial element to court proceedings. Parties work with the court process by putting the negative aspects of their partner into writing and in some ways, it is the one who has the least negative aspects who wins the case.

To understand where lawyers fit in the scheme of things, it is important to step back and examine a court's position in society. Pursuant to Australia's Constitution, State and Commonwealth parliaments enact legislation. Concepts such as "fairness" and "justice" will in part depend on how well the legislation is drafted. Courts determine disputes in accordance with the law (including legislation). This separation of powers is intended to prevent the system from becoming corrupt.

At a basic level, disputing parties go to court. After the evidence has been heard, the judge will give a ruling in accordance with legislation and earlier cases. Under certain circumstances, the parties have a right of appeal to a higher-level court (where the original ruling may be overturned). These decisions (or rulings) of the various courts make up a body of case law – the precedents for future cases.

Future court cases then have the benefit of the written rules (legislation) and the earlier case law. At the risk of oversimplifying the court process, the function of a court is to apply a set of rules to a problem. Criminal law applies rules relating to crime to people's behaviour, civil law provides rules for settling disputes, and family law has rules for families and children. People go to court expecting "justice". At the end of the day the best outcome that hopefully can be achieved is the application of the rules appropriate to the situation.

If you are seeking the courts to be fair, right or just, then you will be disillusioned. All a court can do is apply the rules to a problem. If your evidence fits the rules, then they can act.

The application of the rules is shaped by case law. The judge makes findings and those findings may be appealed. Therefore, the lawyer who advises you becomes important because, even if you read about the legislation relating to family law, how the legislation is applied to your situation may depend upon case law.

From the perspective of a layperson, the Family Court process falls somewhere between an adversarial system and an enquiry system. It is up to the parties to put their information before the court but the judge has the ability to ask some questions. Therefore, not only is a court an alien environment with its own unique rules, it is also a place which is not overly friendly to the average person from the street.

One of the most difficult aspects for those involved in the process (the judge, the lawyers, and ancillary professionals such as court psychologists) is a fundamental deficit in their knowledge with respect to your situation. They were not in your home, they did not see or hear what happened in the relationship, nor have they been there during the break-up. The decision makers are acting on what they are told and they do not have access to the full facts.

Therefore, the people who make the decisions in relation to your children can only consider the facts brought before the court. Parties submit written documents called forms and affidavits which outline the issues. One party submits a log of claims and the other party responds with counter claims. Sometimes independent professionals, such as psychologists, offer opinions in the form of a report. If the case is complicated, an independent children's lawyer may be appointed to deal with the issues. With all of this information a judge has to decide what they believe might be true but, because they were not there, they can only make comments on what they think happened.

The irony of this process is that the court system works backwards (when compared to common sense). The parties file information. This information cannot be tested unless someone is seated in the witness box and is asked a lot of questions about what they have written. The process of testing the evidence in this manner is called a trial. A trial happens towards the end of the court process. Therefore, most of the early decisions of the court are made on an interim basis without the judge being able to find out what has really gone on. Once tested, the court can decide how much weight to put on the material. Until tested, the parties may have to wait for a year or more before they feel their views have been heard.

As the legal process continues, parties seek more and more evidence to "prove" their concerns. Take for example a recent case in which the parents had arguments at the point of handover. One parent got a video camera to show the court what the other parent was doing and saying. The other parent then wanted to cover the bases, so they got one too. The children had to walk from one parent's car into a police station with two video cameras focussed upon them. They then went back to the other parent's car for the drive home.

All of these processes were to serve the purpose of avoiding fights and to prove who was causing the problem (necessary for this couple). However, the children, in the midst of all this, were now being forced into artificial and contrived situations.

The search for substantive evidence can become quite complicated. A parent may get a psychological report. The child is interviewed in the process. A reassessment may be made. Other reports may be requested. One of the worst cases I have been involved with concerned a 10-year-old child who had seen 11 professional people including six psychologists, three psychiatrists and two counsellors. In my opinion, this becomes system abuse. Fortunately, in Australia there are now strict rules which govern how reports may be collected and used in the Family Court, but it does not completely stop this sort of situation.

I have sat through many different trials and have heard comments made by people who have been through the trial process. It is clear there are no winners. Everyone loses. This includes financial losses as well as a perceived loss in terms of the battle for custody. People invest considerable amounts of emotion and time into the legal process. The more they invest the more they have to lose. I have been involved in several cases in which children as young as four have been involved in litigation where both parties have often spent more than $250,000 in combined legal fees. In one complicated and prolonged case the legal bill was over $2 million. Once the parents have gone that far, I do not see how they can back down and reach agreement – they have to keep going until they "win". Where is the child in all this?

At a practical level, papers need to be written, served, filed and processed. Then there are the hearings. It usually takes months between the various steps of the legal process. Often the trial is quite some time down the road. It can take as long as two or three years from when the parties first filed some information to when a judge makes a decision. Cases may go on for many years.

Therefore, the court process is slow, draining and often viewed as not doing anything. When the court does make decisions, people are critical of what is achieved because it was not their preferred solution, nor does the court prove you were the victim and vindicate you of the problems. In my opinion, there are no winners in court, just losers of varying degrees. As I said earlier, the court cannot order people to change their personality so the root problem may never be fixed.

Collaborative law has been created to avoid some of these problems. The way it works is that each parent would have a lawyer so any solution created will ensure that the parties' rights are protected (which is important when trust is low and the implications complex). The lawyers will have signed agreements that they will not represent you in court if the matter does not resolve. This means the lawyers are paid to resolve issues and not go to litigation so it is in everyone's interests to settle the matter.

It is helpful to understand the role of the main players in court. Judges, lawyers and the court will be discussed in the next sections.

Key Points

- When life events happen, whether serious illness, accidents, marriages or the first day at school, children will want and need two parents. Parents need to get it sorted so they can be there when the children really need them.

- Typically, it is a fundamental difference of belief that leads people to separation in the first place. Trying to overcome this difference in an attempt to make the parenting relationship work is very difficult.

- Relationships start as an acquaintance, become a business arrangement (each person does things for the other for practical returns) and then people are intimately associated first as friends and then as lovers. When parents separate, there are negative emotions associated with the break-up which help them to disconnect. These emotions need to be dealt with so the parents can get back to a business level for the sake of the children.

- There are three broad strategies for resolving issues relating to the children:
  1) Reach agreement together.
  2) Mediate a solution with the help of others.
  3) Have a court arbitrate, and in doing so impose a solution.

- The method of reaching solutions will depend on the current state of the relationship. Friends can reach an agreement, business partners may reach agreement or need mediation, while those who are still emotionally disconnecting may need arbitration or mediation.

- The separation process has many cumulative sources of stress which will impact upon a person's life in a variety of different ways. If parents have to use lawyers to settle a dispute, the legal process is a huge additional stress and economic cost.

- Lawyers are necessary to ensure that rights are protected, however, using a lawyer can be akin to opening Pandora's box.

- Collaborative law is a legal strategy which helps reach legal solutions without litigation. It can be a useful avenue to explore.

- There are no winners in court, just losers to varying degrees. In dealing with separation issues in court, you can be right or happy. The harder you try to prove yourself right, the unhappier you will be. If you can let go of the need to be right, then happiness may be possible.

Judges

Judges and magistrates in the Family Court have a terribly difficult job. As I have explained, their job is to apply rules to family situations that they did not directly observe. They did not write the rules but they are bound by the legal process to apply these rules. Orders of the court are usually initially made on an interim basis, because a judge should not make major changes until they have been able to test the information (or unless they have no other choice). Parents may be very worried about a situation that has led them to court in the first place. However, as the judge is not able to test the facts until later, either a conservative position is adopted, or children are left in limbo. The judge has to make cautious decisions in light of safety concerns and untested facts.

The quality of the final judgment is only as good as the facts upon which it was based. The onus is on the parties to get that information before the court. Generally, if someone can afford a lawyer, they will be able to get more information into court than somebody who is self-represented. The lawyer knows the rules and has the skills to present the information to the judge. However, you will never get all the information about your life and relationships to the judge.

The problem for families is that the outcome of the court proceedings will be what a judge thinks is best. One Family Court judge I used to know started his trials by explaining to the parties that if they reached a decision by themselves, they may be a little unhappy (i.e. if they had compromised), but they would be very unhappy if he imposed a solution. He then gave them one last attempt to resolve their problems. The solution imposed by the court is a very important one and therefore I hope judges have all the insight possible, because the child – the precious little life they are making decisions about – will have to live with the consequences for a very long time.

Another irony of the family court system in Australia, is the child, who is the central character in the case, will not appear in court. One of the most sobering aspects of the court process from a parent's point of view, should be the fact the judge, almost always, will never meet your child. Therefore, the judge is making a decision based on the version of the truth presented to the court. A stranger, who does not know or love them, will make decisions in relation to this little person who you have raised and loved.

In my experience, judges are motivated by a genuine desire to do what is best for the children but they are limited in how this may be applied. I hear conspiracy theories claiming collusion by judges and lawyers. While they may know each other, I have not seen it impact their independence.

Key Points

- The person who is making decisions about your children has not met them and does not love them. They can only make decisions based on the information available and the laws that exist at that time.

- The person who makes the decision was not a witness to your relationship. They can only make assumptions about what really happened based on who is the most believable in court. They have no absolute way of finding out the truth.

- The quality of the final judgment is only as good as the facts upon which it was based. The onus is on the parties to get that information before the court, not for the court to find the information.

Lawyers

In our society, there are probably more jokes about lawyers than almost any other profession. People like jokes about lawyers because it is a way of relieving tension in relation to the things we fear. However, once a person is in court, a lawyer becomes a necessity (if you can afford one). Without a lawyer you are handicapped because you will have to deal with an alien system with its own set of rules.

Lawyers vary widely in their style of representation, the stance they take with the issues, and their view as to the best possible outcomes. They range from lawyers who take control of every aspect of the process, to those who do not provide much of their own opinion and want your views only. When selecting a lawyer, it is important you have someone who is prepared to consider the needs of the children in the legal process. I say this because there is a conflict between your instructions to them about what you want, and what is best for the children. The lawyer is obliged to act in accordance with what you want. Having dealt with lawyers for many years, one observation I have made is that some will seek settlement while others will want to take matters to court. You need to find someone you are comfortable with and who will follow your instructions.

Finding a good lawyer is important. I bought a house some years ago. The property had a perimeter fence which was collapsing, but I had not noticed it when I signed the offer to purchase. I rang the settlement agent who said because I had signed the offer to purchase, I would be responsible for the cost of fixing the problem. Not satisfied with that response, I rang a friend of mine, a Family Court lawyer, who said he had a mate who specialised in property law. His mate was then able to indicate a relevant section of the applicable Act, which required external fences to be structurally sound and that the responsibility was the vendor's. This saved me $2000. The bottom line was that neither the settlement agent, nor the family law lawyer, understood the applicable law completely. It is critical you get a specialist.

If you are a Family Court lawyer, I would encourage you to instruct your client about what is best for the children, to enable them to formulate proper instructions to you. This area of law has a unique perspective in that there is a child, who may not have someone representing their interests, involved in the proceedings. Ordinarily, the lawyer's responsibility is to achieve the best outcome for their client. In family separation situations that responsibility may have to be balanced against what is best for the child. In my opinion, there is a moral responsibility of the lawyers involved for the life of the child, who is also in the middle of the conflict.

Key Points

- When selecting a lawyer to appear in the Family Court, it is important a parent has someone who is prepared to consider the needs of the children in the legal process, despite the fact the lawyer must act in their client's best interests.

Children and Court

It is critical that children are kept relatively free from conflict. Parents should not include the children in negotiations, nor ask a child where they would like to live to achieve this. It is not the place of a child under 12 years old to decide what is best for them. That is up to adults. It is imperative children are not told it is their choice unless they have a choice. Once it is written as an order of the court, it is nobody's choice, including the child's or the parents, about what the outcome will be. You have given that responsibility to the judge.

With younger children, the more you question them, the greater the requirement for them to give you an answer. Children who have been pressured will respond by either telling you what you want to hear or taking sides. Therefore, the more you expose the child to the separation issues the worse it will be for the child. There are parents who actively tell young children a great detail about certain issues. I have seen children as young as six years old who have had sections of court documents read to them. The child has been asked where they want to live and whether the other parent is being honest. I find such tactics absolutely appalling. However, even a parent who is highly protective will be less effective in coping with their children if they are involved in the court process.

Children are very astute observers. When the court proceeding comes up and parents become stressed, children will suffer the repercussions by experiencing the distress evident in the house. They may not know what is happening, but they sense the anger, excitement and anxiety. If mum or dad are busy, they may need to write affidavits late at night and therefore they are likely to be tired. It is interesting to hear children tell me they know their parent is going to court because the parent is dressed more formally, the child is sent off to a different relative or friend, or the parents are more stressed and grumpy. The child is aware something is happening. While they may not understand what is happening, the tension does affect them either directly or indirectly.

Parents and other adults need to watch what they say. Talking on the mobile phone, making appointments, talking to lawyers, messages on answering machines etcetera can all be overheard. Children have told me they can hear conversations in the house when in bed trying to sleep. A pair of separated children related how when dad's phone went off it showed "bitch" was calling, and the other one said dad's information on mum's phone was "sperm donor". Therefore, take care to keep information regarding your feelings about your ex-partner and the court proceedings away from children. Being involved in the legal process effectively kills the childhood experience once the little ones become a party to the process.

I prefer to talk about 'big people's business' and 'little people's business' and explain to the child that their business is to be a kid and to have fun, and to let the big people sort out their issues. While this does not resolve the issue, it does help children keep some aspects of their childhood intact.

I have had arguments with parents over their need to tell the children the 'truth'. I believe it is important not to lie to children. However, truth can be like an onion with various layers to be unpeeled. In relation to the court process, it is important children are only shown the very outer layer. They do not need to see the inner layers. Each time you peel back a layer of an onion there are tears. It is the same with the court process.

If you do have to go to court, look for strategies to protect the children, such as keeping children out of the bulk of the conflict, minimising the collection of evidence from them, making sure the people involved in their lives are discreet when talking about issues, and other useful approaches. Protect the child from the dispute – the child is going to be better off in the long run if they are spared the process. I have had a few cases where the children are giving evidence against a parent in a criminal court matter brought by the ex-partner. While it may be their right to press charges, the fact the children end up giving evidence against a parent is alarming. I cannot imagine what the guilt would be like if the parent is convicted and goes to jail – "I put my dad in jail!"

There is some interesting research, although now somewhat dated, which looked at the tendency for parents to "bad mouth" the other side. The study found that children, upon reflection years later, saw the negative parent in a bad light. The study reported that mothers were typically more likely to "bad mouth" than fathers, but given that more children are raised by mothers, and spend longer periods of time with them, there was also more opportunity for it to occur.

One of the best ways to manage the process is through future projection. While going through the court process you need to ask yourself: In 10 or 20 years from now, how will my child look back on what I did at this time? Or alternatively, when they are an adult, will they respect my actions?

Where parents have actively tried to stop children from seeing the other parent, there often comes a time when the child resents the parent who has done that. You do not want to be the product of resentment, nor do you want to be the cause of your child seeking years of therapy as an adult due to their messed-up childhood. You hold half of the situation in your hands – the other half is in the hands of the other party. You need to maximise what you do in your time, and not go tit for tat with the other person.

A current change in the legislation in Australia is for the court to have more of the voice of the children when making decisions. Key people such as the Independent Children's

Lawyer will be talking more to the children about what they want. Please do not contaminate the information by excessively questioning children.

Key Points

- The more a parent exposes the child to separation issues, the worse it will be for the child. Children do not need to know about court.

- Children are very astute observers. Parents and other significant adults need to watch what they say. Talking on the phone, making appointments, talking to lawyers, messages on answering machines etcetera can all be overheard.

- Talking about 'big people's business' and 'little people business' and explaining to the child that their business is to be a kid and to have fun – that is about as much as children need to know about court.

- To help keep your actions in perspective, think in terms of the future. A parent needs to ask themselves in 10 or 20 years from now, how will my child look back on what I did at this time? Or, when the child is an adult, will they respect my actions?

A Voice but Not a Choice

A fundamental issue in the separation process is how much voice a child should be given to the decisions around their life. We live in a time where it is appropriate that children are encouraged to make decisions and learn to speak about what they like. However, some parents lose perspective and, in the process, lose control. For example, a parent ringing-up my office asked my personal assistant, *"What if my child doesn't want to see Dr Watts?"* and my PA replied, "What age is the child?" The parent said *"Four."* I think there is something drastically wrong in the parenting pattern if a parent cannot get a four-year-old into an appointment. Had she said 14, I could perhaps have had some sympathy for her position, although having said that, the only 14-year-olds I have been unable to see are the ones whose parents have presented the process to them in a negative light. To be clear, I believe children should learn to have a voice. However, there are two broad caveats with that which I will explain. The first is the voice needs to be developmentally appropriate, and secondly, in the circumstance of the case, the greater the conflict, the more the voice may be influenced.

Let's return to comments made earlier about brain development. One does not get an adult brain until around age 26. At that age, you are capable of understanding what is best for you, as well as what you would like. At a younger age, children are able to voice what they like with varying degrees of accuracy. It is also important to understand that, as children get older, they have a greater capacity to think about consequences of their decisions, even if they do not have a full adult brain.

Elsewhere in the book I gave the example of a little girl who, when interviewed in my office, spoke highly of visits with her dad but, when returned to the waiting room, put her hands on her hips and said to her mother that she never wanted to see her dad again. This shows the power of influence. In that case, it was an unconscious influence, and the child was effectively reading the mother's anxiety and giving the mother what she wanted.

As a starting point, I would say it is important to consider all children are influenced. Everything parents do has some sort of influence. Some influence may be obvious, such as what a parent says, others may be indirect, such as the child unknowingly listening-in on conversations, and others may be subtle, such as recognising there is a change to their normal routine because something is happening. It is a naïve assumption to assume that, when the child is voicing an opinion, it is a wholly independent view from that child. They are subject to influence.

It is important to understand that children do not think like little adults but have their own unique way of understanding things. As they develop, this thinking changes. For example, children under the age of 10 are typically concrete in their thinking, black-and-white, one parent is right, the other is wrong. Whereas with teenagers there are two sides to every story, and they see things in a very different light.

Children are also big on 'fair'. When they play games they make rules, and sometimes in the 6 to 10-year-old age group they spend more time making the rules than they do actually playing the game. Consequently, if a parent says something is not fair, children will pick up on this. They will argue a certain arrangement is not fair, not because they necessarily understand the implications of the arrangement, but because a parent has alluded to it, for example, *"It's not fair that mummy has more time than daddy."*

As the conflict increases, it becomes harder for a child to be an independent voice. Essentially, in low conflict the views which children express are quite likely to be helpful as they will reflect what they like and are certainly less likely to be influenced. As the conflict increases, the children may be able to provide some useful information, but they are also likely to be trying to survive. As explained elsewhere, children are ingenious survivors and will say things to parents as a coping mechanism. As the conflict gets more severe, a child is more likely to come up with firmly expressed views, but with less ability for it to reflect their true position. Essentially, what I am saying is the greater the conflict, the less reliance should be put on the voice of the child.

I get quite frustrated when a parent says, *"My child doesn't want to see the other parent, therefore, they shouldn't have to."* If the child was refusing to go to school, you would be doing everything you possibly could to make them go by trying to work out what the problem was and how to encourage them to go. However, when it comes to an ex-partner, people seem to be satisfied to simply go, *"They don't want to go, therefore, I'm not going to make them."*

When asking children about different arrangements, it is important to realise children often like what they have got because it is familiar. They often have problems determining what it may be like in a different arrangement. Sometimes it is helpful if changes are trialled so they can be evaluated afterwards as a 'lived' experience and determined if it is workable. For example, I saw two children, one 17 and one 10. The 17-year-old wanted to live with one parent while she was doing her final exams, the other child believed she would be happy doing week-about. However, three months after doing the week-about, she realised she missed her sister and preferred to have a greater proportion of time in the house where her sister was residing. She could not imagine this beforehand.

I presented at a conference under the heading "A Voice, Not a Choice". The reason I said this is I believe children should have a voice and be able to express what they like and why they like it. However, ultimately, the big people need to decide what is best in a child's life, and children should not be given the illusion it is their decision. To choose to see or not see a parent is a very heavy burden and, if there is conflict, the children may well be saying it for a whole lot of reasons which are not valid, and they will carry the regret and guilt of what they said through their life.

Key points

- Children, even young children, can tell us useful information about what they like, and they should be heard.

- Even older children lack the brain development to fully understand the implications about what is best for them. Their wishes should not be over-valued.

- Children say things for a lot of reasons, and unless you can understand the context and the pressure on them, you may miss the meaning of what they are saying.

- The bottom line is children should have a voice, but ultimately not the choice.

Mediation and Friendship

When parents are in the process of separating, except when it is by mutual agreement to separate, and particularly in the first two years, it is difficult to see each other without emotions arising. Agreement can only be reached if the significant levels of emotions are managed, whether that is the sadness or anger. If your emotions are out of control, or if your emotional objectivity is coloured, it may not be wise to meet face-to-face (at least initially). Email or text allows you time to think through your answers, rather than just reacting on the spur of the moment.

Can I also suggest that stop, breathe, think, act should be your mantra before sending any email or text. Pause so you do not react. Take a couple of deep calming breaths to regain focus. Think about the implications of the action. Will this help you achieve your goals or make it harder? Is it repair or damage? If possible, have someone review your important emails and texts before you send them. That way you do not cause further damage.

In the long run, the best way to deal with problems between you and your former partner is to sit down, have a cuppa, talk over the issues in a friendly, non-threatening way and try to reach an agreement. Some couples will never be able to achieve this ideal due to their mismatched personalities. The bitterness of the court proceedings may also make this option less likely. However, if I present the ideal to strive for, anything closer to it will help your children.

In the process of the face-to-face negotiation, it is important to remember the progression from acquaintance to business partner, to friend, to lover is a relatively natural transition. The transition from being a romantic partner to that of 'just friends' is an unnatural progression because you have to 'unexperience' levels of intimacy which friends would not have normally have experienced. Time heals most things, and years later it may be possible to achieve that level.

As touched on earlier, while waiting for the hurt to settle, the best option is to think about the children as a business. You and the ex-partner are business associates with the job of raising children. Therefore, the two of you need to get together to discuss the business and keep away from any discussion of the topics related to the failed previous relationship. The more strictly you stick to the business the better.

In the early period of trying to re-establish a relationship, having an agenda can be a useful strategy. Write down what you want to discuss, have the other party agree to that, and then meet to discuss it. If either of you stray from the topic, bring it back to that agenda, leaving other issues for next time. This tends to limit the parties from straying into difficult areas. It allows both parents to think about what they want prior to the meeting.

If you are unable to keep control of your discussions, the next option is to find an independent mediator. This is somebody who can function as a dampener on the heat of the discussion. For example, the lowest level of mediator could be a trusted person who you both agree to – a mutual friend, trusted family member, or somebody else who is willing to get involved. Obviously, there are lower costs and other benefits associated with using friends or family. If it can work, it is a useful option and often quick to get into place. However, it may not be suitable if you cannot agree as to who should do it or if the animosity is too high, in which case you need a professional. Generally speaking, the fewer external people involved in the situation the better, but mediation by family may not always be a good idea, especially if that person also has issues about your break-up.

There are formal mediators available. These people may have psychological or legal training, but a qualified mediator must also be trained in the process of mediation. A formal mediator is trained to help parties reach resolution (not to resolve underlying issues). If the two of you cannot talk to each other, and it is not appropriate to use an agreed third party, then seek the services of a recommended accredited formal mediator.

From my perspective, there are advantages to using both legally trained and psychologically trained mediators. What really matters is that you have someone with whom both of you can talk, who can control the process and keep the two of you on task. Sometimes a series of mediations is helpful for the two of you to re-establish rules, whereby you can then continue working out the issues by yourselves.

The most important aspect in relation to mediation is to see to the priorities of the children in particular, therefore making sure your issues and concerns are put on the agenda and resolved. I would point out that mediation can take a fair amount of time, especially if animosity is high. It is better not to cease mediation early, even if the process does not seem to be getting anywhere. Sometimes the gains are gradual.

Another strategy is the use of parenting coordinators. In the United States they are common while in Australia it is a relatively rare service. What a coordinator does is not so much act as a mediator but as an arbitrator. They advise you both on the best course of action for the decision at hand. In the US, the coordinator can be backed by legal authority (they make binding decisions), while in Australia, judicial authority cannot be delegated so it requires both parties to accept the decision.

In the long term, it is important to have multiple avenues of communication, especially for children's issues. Mediation involves some form of face-to-face discussion and, if formal mediation is needed, many of the little day-to-day issues may not be able to be addressed. Therefore, having a communication book, which goes in the children's bags, to outline current concerns, is a useful strategy. However, in this day and age of email, SMS and apps it is possible to transfer messages easily. What is not beneficial is to get children, particularly younger children, to verbally convey the messages. This puts them in the middle of the parents.

The bottom line is that you and your former partner are going to have to reach agreement on both big and small issues. Issues such as who the child should live with and how much time they should have with the other parent, through to how many pairs of socks they should have, which school to attend, should they play Aussie Rules or soccer, ballet or netball, and so on. The sooner you can establish a bridge of communication, the better for everyone, especially the children.

The downside of a court proceeding is that the bridge of communication tends to get worse, not better, as litigation escalates. Therefore, I strongly urge the two of you to resolve problems on a face-to-face basis initially, if that is at all possible. If not, seek to mediate. An arbitrated solution needs to be seen as a solution of last resort. Having spent more than 30 years involved with the court system it would still be my last resort. It is not because it is excruciatingly slow to reach a decision, not because it is outrageously expensive to maintain legal representation, although both of these are true. It is because I would not trust something as important as the wellbeing of my children to a stranger unless I had no other option.

In conflict resolution there is a strategy called the "least to most principle". This principle works along the lines of starting with the least disruptive strategy – you can always escalate, but you can never go back. For example, if you try the friendly approach and it does not work, you can seek mediation, and then eventually go to court. However, once you have been in the court forum, it is very hard to go back to talking on friendly terms because of the damage done.

A principle I have recommended to a number of people who have sought counselling from me as they have gone through the court process is to 'kill your partner with kindness'. Many want to kill their partners, but not with kindness. Given the level of animosity, the natural tendency is to fight and fight hard. However, the more you seek to do nice things, the more you try to be helpful, the greater the likelihood they will reciprocate in the long term. The old fashion golden rule – do unto others as you would have done unto you – is sound advice for parents, not just for children.

I accept there are some people with whom it is impossible to mediate or negotiate, and there ultimately needs to be arbitration. However, I believe a proportion of those cases in the Family Court, where a judge makes the decision, could have had a different outcome. If the parties had chosen a different beginning, the ending would have also been different. This is reflected in part by the federal government's attempts to set up mediation centres to assist couples in conflict resolution. I certainly applaud any effort that intervenes early and keeps couples talking. There is a place for a court system, but the more you can avoid going there, the better for all of you, especially your children.

Key Points

- Parents need to see themselves as business associates with their job being that of raising children. The more strictly parents stick to the "business" the better it will be for everyone.

- In conflict resolution there is a strategy called the "least to most principle". This principle works by starting with the least disruptive strategy, because it is possible to escalate a situation, but it is often not possible to go back. If you try mediation, you can always go to court later, but it is much harder the other way around.

- Just as organisations do in the business world, an agenda can be a useful strategy for parents. Write down the points to be discussed, have the other party agree to the points of discussion, and then meet to discuss them. If either party strays from the topic, bring the discussion back to the agenda, leaving other issues for next time.

- If you are unable to keep control of your discussions, the next option is to find a mediator. An informal level of mediation involves the use of a mutual friend, church leader, or someone else you both can rely on. If it helps, great, but it may make the issues more complicated.

- The government has opened family centres to help separating couples, while various non-government organisations provide mediation. Having a professional mediator who is trained and independent can be beneficial.

- At the risk of complicating matters, a mediated solution may also include legal considerations because most mediators are not necessarily trained in law.

- The old-fashioned principle of doing to others what you would have others do to you is a really good way of breaking down barriers. A principle that I recommend is to 'kill your partner with kindness'. Be nice, if for no other reason than for your own self-respect.

Assertiveness and Other Myths

Communication with your ex-partner is tricky. When feelings are high people react. In the previous section I have outlined the need to think about your decisions and to act in a manner which allows you to control your emotions. To give a simple example, the ex-partner brings the children home late again. Uncensored reactions may go something like, *"You are late again, you inconsiderate prick."* This is an invitation to fight. Blaming, name calling and anger are a volatile mix. Hopefully you will have considered the previous section and only FELT like saying this but did not actually send the message! There are ways to do better.

As a clinical psychologist seeing parents for marriage communication, I used to teach them how to use assertive communication. Assertiveness is a staple tool in the psychologist's toolbox. ABC – antecedents, behaviour, consequence. The process is to explain the trigger (the antecedents), by identifying the behaviours (behaviours) and then explaining the consequences (the consequences) while doing it in a friendly way.

A *"You said you would be home at 5pm, you came at 5:30."* – This is a good antecedent in that it is very specific and hard to argue.

B *"This made me feel worried and stressed."* These are your feelings and it is hard to argue you don't feel that.

C *"Either bring them home as agreed and I can be calm, or bring them home late and I may become irrational and angry".* Two consequences based on the behaviour of the person.

For a lot of people assertive communication is very helpful. It allows them to say what they need. Learning to say "I feel" (owning feelings) rather than "you are" (blaming) significantly improves communication. It is especially helpful within a relationship which you value. If you do not know how to communicate in this manner, then practise this and look up a workbook on how to do it better. It is an excellent way to communicate in a relationship.

However, when I was teaching this to people who were in family court situations, I found a steady stream of people reporting it did not work, or when they did use it the opposite happened. If you look carefully at the steps, you will see why it may not work when you are dealing with someone who no longer cares about you and may be feeling angry toward you. It is especially bad if they have a personality disorder or some other type of pathology. *"I feel"* – *well I don't care about how your feelings*. Give a consequence – *don't you dare tell me what to do*. Using the scenario above:

A *"You said you would be home at 5pm you came at 5:30."* – We were not late. I didn't agree to that time, you made it to control me.

B *"This made me feel worried and stressed."* – Who cares what you feel! You are just neurotic. Or even worse, if they want to push your buttons you have just told them how to do it, and some nasty people will actually now deliberately do it more.

C *"Either bring them home as agreed and I can be calm, or bring them home late and I may become irrational and angry."* – How dare you try to control me by telling me what to do.

In other words, the process of setting in place assertive boundaries has gone completely pear shaped. The psychologist you were consulting told you this and it is not working. It can be easy to then start thinking psychology does not work or you are a failure. I can tell you the reason it did not work had more to do with the nature of the dynamics than your efforts. Without the incentive of the relationship, some people no longer care about your emotions, nor do they want to agree. For some people a bad relationship is still a relationship, and they enjoy being in the position of causing problems.

Bill Eddy of the High Conflict Institute, has a model of communication for these types of situations which is not an assertiveness model. When I read about it, it rang very true for the population I am dealing with. He developed a model called

BIFF. The BIFF form of communication is not guaranteed to work but it has a better chance of working than the assertiveness.

BIFF stands for Brief, Informative, Firm and Friendly. "The children were later than we agreed. To keep things moving smoothly please ensure they come at the agreed time." What this does not contain is any feelings, especially anger. It minimises control. It sets a boundary but does not try to enforce it. You will get a lot further using BIFF than assertiveness with a difficult ex-partner. Bill Eddy has a book called *BIFF for Co-Parent Communication: Your Guide to Difficult Texts, Emails and Social Media Posts*. It is well worth the read.

The final point I would raise is that when communication is struggling, there are many things you can do to make it worse but very few will make it better. BIFF is a technique which may not get your result but lowers the likelihood of the situation getting worse.

Key Points

- Reactive communication will only lead to escalation of problems. You need to control your reactions and emotions.

- Assertiveness is a staple tool in the psychologist's toolbox. ABC – antecedents, behaviour, consequence. The process is to explain the trigger (the antecedents), by identifying the behaviours (behaviours) and then explaining the consequences (the consequences). This works well when you and your ex-partner respect each other.

- Assertiveness often does not work when people are separated.

- BIFF communication as proposed by Bill Eddy has a style of communication which lowers emotions and reactions. It stands for Brief, Informative, Firm and Friendly. Highly recommended for communication with ex-partners, especially difficult ones.

Strategy and Boundaries

Separated families can quickly deteriorate into turf wars. There are arguments over potentially everything. It is important to understand the need for boundaries with an ex-partner. This is complicated as everything can change; where a couple used to both be able to walk into the house whenever they wanted before separation, after separation they should knock and start respecting the space. Note the word "should". "Should" may not happen unless someone says something. Therefore, unless you explain the new rules and boundaries, it may not happen. Same with almost everything the couple does. The sooner the boundary is set the better.

When boundaries are being put in place it is common for the other party to push back. It is important to understand this and get it right. Too hard boundaries escalate tension and make it unnatural for the children. For example, doing a handover at McDonald's or a police station. Therefore, unless it is necessary, do not set the boundaries higher than is needed. The level should be set according to risk and dynamic. If you can do the handover at the front door then it is more natural for the children.

Note that if you have always done something and now you stop it, the other person will feel ripped off even if what you were doing was extreme. Better to have the boundary right to start with than change it later. Couple with this is a simple principle. If you knock twice on a door and get no answer, what do you do? The answer is knock louder. If nothing happens you walk away. However, if they come after the third knock, what are you going to do next time? Knock at least three times, the last couple very loudly. Same with change. If you normally get your way and now you don't, you will try to get it by doing what you have always done. New boundaries will see an increase in resistance before being established as the new normal. Don't forget that. Either give in early or stand your ground, don't give in halfway. While this is a good principle for dealing with an ex it is also an important principle as a parent.

When deciding on how to deal with issues think about the shotgun and sniper approaches. If you fire at every issue people retreat to their bunker. Lawyers like boundaries and escalate the conflict by taking on all the issues. This is the shotgun approach. The sniper approach is to make a plan and let go everything which is not in the plan. For example, in the Family Court, if the goal is more access to the children, the ex-partner arriving 10 minutes late could be made an issue, but it is more strategic to let it go as it will not help the overall goal. The key is to pick your battles and do not fight over everything.

How you communicate is very important. The quickest way to upset someone is to wind them up by name calling. For example, if you call them a narcissist or tell them they have borderline personality disorder they will not turn around and say, *"Thank you for that diagnosis, it is so helpful!"* They will rage. If they do have one of those personality disorders they are going to feel wounded and want revenge; if they do not they are insulted and want revenge. The same can be said for any *"you are..."* statements. Try using some of the following examples to lower conflict.

> Do not say, *"You are wrong."* Use terms like, *"I see it differently."*
>
> Words like, *respect* and *value your opinion,* are worth their weight in gold.
>
> Do not tell them you are leaving them – abandonment can trigger rage or wound a sense of entitlement.

A principle I like when dealing with high conflict people is the illusion of control. This is about shaping their thinking. If you make a suggestion, they will reject it. However, if it is their idea, they support it. Therefore, wait until they come up with something close to what you want, then compliment them on the good idea. This then shapes their thinking, so you eventually get what you wanted, but it is their idea. It takes a bit of practice and patience, but it can work quite well.

I would note that some of these strategies are the opposite to what is suggested by well-meaning professionals. They may say set firm boundaries, and may encourage you to tell your ex-partner how it is going to be. You may be told to not give an inch. Such approaches elevate conflict and risk. Of course, you have to work with the advice you are paying to get, but in my opinion, it is so much better to be controlled and patient with a heavy dose of strategy. I like the sniper approach. Bide your time, ignore any issue which is not central, and let them put their guard down. This means longer periods of smoother sailing. You can then shoot them at close range (figuratively not literally) on the issues which really matter.

It is useful to think about the words of TV's Dr Phil who once said that you can be right or happy. With an ex-partner who likes conflict, the more right you try to be the less happy you will become. It is important to weigh up the cost of the conflict on your mental wellbeing.

I will leave this section with a sobering thought: there are some people who enjoy conflict, and watching you suffer may be the very thing they are aiming for. Therefore, avoid giving pleasure to them by not letting them see you suffer, and do not fight them for things which really do not matter.

Key Points

- The higher the conflict from your ex-partner the greater the need to be strategic in your approach.

- Set and keep boundaries but be thoughtful in how and when you set them.

- Try the sniper style of dealing with issues. This means being strategic rather than jumping on everything you disagree with.

- The illusion of control can be extremely helpful in getting things your way. You have to give up the ownership of the idea and allow your ex-partner to take credit for the idea. The reward is you get the outcome you were hoping to achieve.

- Avoid name calling. Telling someone what you think they are is only going to serve to make them angrier at you.

- TV's Dr Phil once said you can be right or happy. What do you want? Trying to prove you are right will only inflame the conflict and you will not be happy.

5

Shared Care and Other Options

The sad aspect of parental separation is that the situation for children and, in most cases parents, will be irrevocably altered in ways which mean the parents generally have less opportunity for quality time with their children. You have to let go of the hope and expectations from the past and accept you are creating something new. In the words of my young adult son, "You have to accept that it is what it is."

I am firmly of the opinion children do best with two parents who get on and can work together within a relationship and anything else is a compromise. Now that you have separated, you need to work out the best compromise situation you can. This section is about developing the arrangement for the children which will serve them the best. You can only do this by looking forward to what you are creating and not to the past and what you might have had. You also need to realise you have an ideal family and a real family. The ideal of what you want may be gone, but you still have a real family to work with.

As explained earlier, in a functioning family, two parents are each capable of being with their children to a maximum of 100 per cent of the time, accounting for a total parental involvement of 200 per cent. Obviously, with demands of life such as work, school, housework, social activities and so on, the full quota will never be achieved. Separation effectively halves the maximum possible time spent with children, while the demands of life will often increase. In an equal shared care arrangement, each parent is going to have half of the maximum time available, in other words 50 per cent of the available time. Therefore, unless one parent disappears totally, each parent suffers a loss. Each parent will grieve the loss of some of the former involvement in the lives of the children. It is the hardest emotional cost of the whole separation for most parents.

The optimal situation for a child's development is to have two parents available – everything else is a compromise. To help children get what is best for them, the obvious priority is to seek help to fix the relationship, deal with the issues and not separate. Where that is not possible, alternative regimes need to be considered and parents have to realise they will have much less opportunity with the children than before separation.

In any arrangement which does not involve half the time with each parent, one parent will have significantly fewer opportunities, although ratios will vary. This may reflect the type of relationship which existed previously. For example, some mine workers may work four weeks on/one week off and may have only been present for a small percentage of the child's time while the other parent has had the larger percentage. The norm, however, is likely to have been that either one, or both parents, worked and both had a combination of afterhours and weekend time with the children. In families still able to afford the luxury of having one income earner and one stay at home parent, the share of time will be larger for one than the other. However, the traditional family structure is less frequently seen now.

In the past, the Family Court has put a lot of weight on maintaining the status quo. In other words, what was happening before separation continued after separation unless there was an overwhelming reason to change the arrangement. Underpinning this psychologically is the fact that time and attachment are loosely related. The new arrangements retained the arrangements of what had gone before, acting as legal buffer for the children. With the new legislation, the Family Court has proposed an alternative method for dealing with the issues based on what is best for the children. This means the court does not have to be bound by the past but rather must do what is best for the child. Therefore, this means any number of arrangements may be suitable from the court's point of view, and the attachment aspect may not be maintained. Therefore, all parents need to consider the fact that they will not have their old life anymore, and the court will not simply continue what has gone before.

In relation to time with children, it is important to realise there will generally be less time available after separation. The more acrimonious the relationship break-up, the less flexibility there will be to see the children at other times. It is not possible to pop in to see the children, call to say goodnight, take them out on a day off and so forth if there are restraining orders and court specified visiting regimes. With acrimony, the time will increasingly become blocks of contact and periods of no involvement – an arrangement which is opposite to that in which children are normally raised, where they have frequent contact of varying lengths with both parents.

Where parents have a co-operative arrangement, they may be able to pop around and see the children for a few hours here and there in addition to regular blocks of time, thus approximating the normal arrangement. The more acrimonious the relationship, the less possibility in this regard. Flexibility is providence of good relationships. Furthermore, this type of opportunity becomes less feasible as each parent re-partners. As an ongoing pattern, it becomes more intrusive on the various relationships. Therefore, flexibility between even the most co-operative parents will have its limitations as time goes on.

In the early part of the break-up, people sometimes go around to the other partner's home, using the guise of seeing the children, when the real motive is to see the ex-husband or wife. This mixing of issues is a recipe for disaster. Keep the motives pure or it will lead to problems. If you are going to see the children, spend the time with the children. If you want to talk to the partner, ring them up and make a time when the children are not around. The children and your ex-partner do not need mixed messages.

When considering the different possibilities for arrangements, it is important to weigh up whether the arrangements under consideration are being proposed on the basis of what is fair for parents or what is best for children. While it may be hard to separate the issues, remaining focused on the children is essential if they are to maximise their ability to cope with the separation process.

This leads to the next significant consideration: the type of arrangement which is going to be best for the children. This relates to the issue of the parents' capacity to function in a healthy manner. There is a percentage of the population who, for intellectual, emotional, personality or psychiatric reasons, are more limited in their capacity. They may also have made lifestyle choices, particularly in relation to substance abuse, which impair functioning. Therefore, there may need to be fewer opportunities with the children but in the process balance the benefit by periods of good quality contact. The damage, which can be caused by inadequate or inappropriate parents, needs to be limited. In cases where the question of a parent's capacity comes to light, it is likely a professional assessment will be required because these cases are difficult to resolve. Professional advice in relation to what is best for the children is often a necessary balancing act in which various factors have to be traded off.

As an aside, I would also point out that generic professional advice may not be sufficient to address these issues adequately. Child psychologists, paediatricians, psychiatrists and other professionals may have a lot of good advice to offer. However, the impact of various factors on children in conflicted separated families may require additional specialist expertise. It is important to ensure the professional has experience in dealing with complex family break-ups, not just experience in children's issues.

Practical considerations are particularly important when considering arrangements involving children. There is a greater flexibility in situations where parents live close to each other. The following examples illustrate the type of situations that can occur. I was involved in a case where one of the partners relocated from a country town to the city. The parents had previously had a shared care arrangement from time of the birth of their child, in which they had a week-about arrangement. The matter had come to me for a professional assessment because the child was about to commence school. A 230km one-way journey made it necessary to resolve the schooling issues. A similar case involved two parents who lived at opposite ends of the metropolitan area. One of the parents proposed a shared care arrangement but wanted the child to be enrolled in two different schools. The moment parents consider putting their child into two different schools, the issue of the child's best interest has been lost. The final example concerned a father who worked offshore on a three week on/three week off cycle. He proposed a 50:50 shared care arrangement, resulting in three-week blocks of time with each parent. It was simply not viable for their young children to be put into such a large rotational cycle.

There are many practical issues to consider in relation to the best interests of the child, such as the need for the child to have friends nearby. A child who goes to school in one area, but has recreational time in a different area, will have no local peer network and may have difficulty going to parties or playing sport. I had a case in which the parents had a three day/four day shared arrangement but lived about an hour apart. The father had the child on every weekend, and the mother had Monday to Thursday nights. The child had soccer training on Wednesday but played matches on Saturday. Should the child be enrolled in a club near mum or near dad? It would be far better for the parents to live closer together. Someone was going to have to travel each week. In this case the child went to soccer with dad. However, when mum had a new baby, she could no longer commit to the travel.

Parenting desires and motivation are also important considerations. It is necessary to ask yourself some soul-searching questions to determine what your particular desires truly are, and to what degree your current feelings are a product of the separation situation. There are some parents who, because of their career aspirations, lifestyle commitments or other factors, are really best suited to seeing their children on a periodic basis and are happy for this not to be a significant amount of time. I recently assessed an executive who worked in the city but frequently travelled overseas. He was quite willing to settle for an arrangement in which he had the children for approximately five days a month. The complicating factor was that this needed to be on an irregular basis, rather than on a regular cycle. While the children may miss out on time with their dad, he was realistic about his work commitments. Conversely, another working father, who demanded 50 per cent care, put the children into before and after-school care from 7am to 6pm. Ironically, when one of the children developed a blood condition which required three visits to the hospital a week, this man (who had argued he was capable of providing the care) had the mother take the child to hospital in both his and her weeks as he did not want to take time off work. The literature still shows that care is not equal even on 50:50 arrangements. The research shows that typically the mother is likely to have more days off looking after a sick child than the father.

There are many practical problems associated with shared care. A large physical distance between houses certainly creates a lot of problems. However, a divided care attitude creates problems even if parents live close together. In one case, where the parents lived three houses apart, the children were not allowed to see the other parent outside of the prescribed times. It is common in the more serious Family Court cases to hear of children, when they see their other parent in a shopping centre, park or some other venue, not being allowed to talk to that parent. While I understand that even brief contact may bring up issues for the parent, it creates major confusion and turmoil from the child's perspective.

On the positive side, one of the most successful shared care cases I assessed involved a boy aged 11 who lived in suburb divided by a park. He could cycle from one home to the next in under five minutes. Although he lived in a week-about arrangement, his mum started work early so he went to his dad before school, and his dad worked until 5.30pm so he went to his mother after school. On weekends he could go where he wanted to as long as both parents were told which home he was supposed to be in. Therefore, irrespective of who he was with, he saw his mum and dad every day. The parents living close to each other had good communication, and by allowing the child to have choice, enabled this lad to have a real shared care life. Such sharing is only possible because these people trusted and respected each other as parents.

In my fantasy moments I think about how I would like to see parents arguing less in court about time and more in psychologist offices about how to get trust and respect back. Ultimately, it is not the time but the respect between parents which has the greatest positive impact on the children.

Key Points

- Separation means children will get less time with their parents and parents will get less time with their children. All miss out. If parents want an alternative, then they need to fix the relationship.

- It is critical the outcome is based on what is best for the children, not what is fair for the parents. It is the child, not the parent, who should be at the centre of the decisions.

- The more acrimonious the relationship break-up, the less flexibility there will be to see the children at other times. It is not possible to call in to see the children, to call to say goodnight, or take them out on a day off and so forth.

- Parents need to keep their motives pure when dealing with the former partner, otherwise problems will ensue. If they are going to see the children, they need to spend the time with the children and not try to resolve issues with the ex.

- Practical considerations are particularly important when making arrangements involving children. There is greater flexibility where parents live close to each other.

- It is necessary for parents to ask themselves some soul-searching questions to determine what their desires truly are. There are some parents who, because of their career aspirations, lifestyle commitments or other factors, are really best suited to seeing their children on a periodic basis.

- The child's life becomes divided as co-operation fails and acrimony increases. Shared care is based on co-operation.

Children's Factors in Parenting Arrangements

The first thing to consider before choosing any parenting arrangement is the age of the children. The younger the child, the greater the requirement for shorter, more frequent visits to keep the parents in the child's psychological world. Out of sight quickly becomes out of mind for very young children.

Our perceptions of time change as we mature. For example, and as a simple way of trying to understand this concept, at 17 years of age I took out a small loan for a motorbike. The loan was for a period of 12 months, and it seemed like a frighteningly long period to be committed to making regular payments. At 26 years of age, I had my first mortgage (for a term of 30 years). I was less anxious about the latter period of time than I had been about the 12-month loan. As a mature adult we can see people once a year and still maintain a relationship. For young children the requirement is based on weeks and, for infants and babies, the requirement in building a strong relationship needs to be short, frequent intervals generally no more than days between visits.

Within the Family Court domain and associated professional literature, the age at which overnight visitation should commence is an area of controversy. Generally speaking, there are two broad lines of argument. The first argument states that even very young children cope with overnight contact and that it is a very useful bonding experience for the parents. It helps the parents to have a meaningful relationship with the child, and helps the child develop a sense of security with the parent. The counter argument tends to focus on attachment issues. It recognises, as the psychological literature shows, that secure attachment comes from having a stable base and that attachment damage should be avoided at all costs. Therefore, the argument to delay the onset of overnight contact until the child is older is a serious and significant consideration. A key point is what was the arrangement before separation. A couple who fell pregnant and were never together will need a different arrangement to a couple who both helped care for the child for her first year of life.

For the social scientist, there is great difficulty in conducting research about the effect of parental separation on children under the age of two or three. Therefore, there may never be a definitive answer to these issues. What we do know, however, is that from birth to six months of age a frequent and predictable visitation pattern is recommended. The more frequently the non-custodial parent can be available (and the more available prior to separation) the longer the duration should be. It is therefore recommended there be visits of three to five times a week for two to three hours duration. Ideally, these sorts of arrangements should provide opportunities for feeding and bathing the child as this can help build up the trust relationship between the child and parent. For infants, who can be visited only once or twice a week, visitation should not exceed two or three hours. Where a child can be visited four or five times a week, the duration can be longer.

In the 6 to 12-month age group visitation arrangements depend on how much prior contact they have had. If they had little prior contact, visitation should be short and frequent. Between the ages of 18 months to three or four years, children can handle less frequent visits than infants, but consistency and frequency are still very important. Visits of a lengthy duration are not recommended. The exact length of time for a child of this age is not known. My rule of thumb for block contact for children between the ages of three and six years is one night for every year of age (i.e. a three-year-old would have approximately three nights, and a six-year-old could have a week away from their primary attachment parent). Block contact is not regular contact, but periods of time associated with special occasions.

In the age range of 12 months to three years, the issue of overnight contact has been hotly debated within the profession. Some authors recommend that overnight contact is quite appropriate, while other authors argue against it. On my reading of the literature, for children under the age of 12 months, overnight contact is not advisable unless the parents have shown a well-documented pre-existing basis of caring for the infant and the arrangements were established very early in the child's life. If the parents have a really good relationship, it may be better for the infant to keep the child in the home and change the parent instead (see nesting below).

The time at which overnight contact begins, in my opinion, depends largely on the strength of the relationship between the child and the parents. I certainly recommend that by the time a child is three years old they should be capable of regular overnight visits with the alternate parent. I then recommend that this frequency increase so that by the time the child is six years old they are capable, if it is appropriate, of a significant shared care arrangement. This can be quite hard for a parent who separates when their child is very young, say 12 months of age, to gradually build up the sharing arrangement until the child is six years old. I understand their frustration, however it is a case of working out what is best for the child, rather than satisfying the parents' own needs.

In making recommendations for overnight contact for children under three years of age, the strength of the relationship between the child and the parent is paramount. The second factor of particular significance, in my opinion, is the degree of co-operation between parents. For example, if the parents have a co-operative relationship, and if the child has a bad night, they are still able to seek comfort from their primary parent. If the parties are capable of facilitating this, then overnight contact is appropriate for children at the younger end of the age scale. However, if parents are going to stick with rigidly adhered to schemes, then this flexibility is not possible, and the child may not be best served by having overnight contact at this stage.

I was involved with a case where the father said the three-year-old coped with the three- night blocks when overnight started. However, when I interviewed the paternal grandmother, she was saying how terrible it was to hear the little girl crying herself to sleep every night. The dishonestly of the parent to win the court case was costing the little girl her sense of safety. It would have been easier and better to have been honest, cut the time back until the child was ready, then introduce the increased time.

I have frequently noted an interesting development with two to three-year-olds. Children may have established overnight contact, with a period of running quite smoothly up to the age of two years old. But then somewhere around 2½ years of age, the child suddenly becomes reluctant to go on visits and shows a range of distress behaviours (including crying, hiding, hanging onto objects, as well as stating they do not want to go on visits).

The alternate parent in these situations may report that when the child comes to them, they arrive upset but quickly settle. This phenomenon relates to an attachment process where the child is consolidating a primary attachment and is distressed at leaving. In ideal circumstances overnight contact should be reduced for a time (i.e. months) while the frequency of shorter visits is increased, the relationship rebuilt, and then the overnight contact reintroduced, ideally around the age of three.

It is important to separate this behaviour from that of a child who is genuinely distressed about something happening in the other home. For example, I saw one child who was being bullied by a jealous stepsibling. A clue to the problem includes the child consistently complaining of some problems which is not short-lived (usually over within six months). I can envisage some significant problems in cases where a shared care arrangement of a week-about is enforced by the court over this period. Rather than being a transient issue, it may damage the child's sense of security in the world.

With young children, the best arrangements are those where there is a stable primary base with visits to the other parent's home. In the under three-year-olds, if overnight visits are introduced, I prefer to recommend one or two separate overnight stays per week, not consecutive nights. This allows the child a recharge cuddle with the primary attachment figure.

Where there is a group of siblings, and one of them is younger, often the youngest child can cope with longer periods because they have siblings. However, if the other siblings are taking parental responsibility and are looking after the younger siblings, this would not be in any of the children's best interests. Also, it may be the case that if one child is particularly young

Shared Care and Other Options 213

in comparison to their siblings, a separate arrangement for the youngest child may be necessary.

With children under three years old, I am strongly opposed to week-about arrangements. If any arrangement is to be put in place, I would recommend either a two/two/three-night cycle run over a fortnight (so each parent has blocks of three days over a weekend) or a three day/four-day cycle to ensure both parents are seen frequently. I also recommend, if it is possible, that each parent sees the child each day, even if for a brief time (at least until the child reaches two years of age). Similarly, I am opposed to visits of alternate nights or arrangements where the child has days with one parent and nights with other (i.e. 12-hour cycles). This chopping and changing is difficult for all but a very easy-going, stable child to cope with.

To summarise my recommendations in relation to younger children, overnight contact should not start before the age of 12 months unless there has been a well-established high degree of shared care in the pre-existing relationship and the child has demonstrated a strong attachment to both parents (generally speaking overnight contact is preferable after 12 months). Somewhere between the ages of 12 months and three years, overnight contact should be introduced. The timing should be related to the readiness of the child. Ideally, overnight contact should not be longer than a single block of up to 24 hours when first introduced. If there is a strong pre-existing relationship, overnight contact of twice a week, but not on consecutive days, may be viable. If that is not viable, two afternoon periods and a block of 24 hours would be a workable compromise where there is some degree of reticence between the parties. By way of example, if one parent is working, an arrangement can be made consisting of after-work visits for a few hours on two afternoons, with overnight stays on the weekend. In cases where there is intense animosity between the parents, I would recommend delaying the onset of overnight contact until the child is around three years of age, especially because of the behavioural problems which may show up at the age of 2½ years.

Key Points

- The better the parents relate to each other, and the more secure the child is with both parents, the greater the options for a young child.

- Birth to six months – a frequent and predictable visitation pattern is recommended. The more frequently the non-custodial parent can be available (and the more available prior to separation) the longer the duration should be. It is recommended that there be visits of four or five times a week for two to three hours duration. For infants, who can be visited only once or twice a week, visitation should not exceed two or three hours.

- In the 6 to 12-month age group, visitation arrangements depend upon how much prior contact they have had. If they had little prior contact, visitation should be short and frequent.

- The age at which overnight visitation should commence for young children is an area of controversy. There are two main arguments, the second of which I tend to support more strongly:

1) Young children cope with overnight contact and it is a very useful bonding experience for the parents. It helps the parents to have a meaningful relationship with the child, and helps the child develop a sense of security with the parent.

2) The counter argument tends to focus on attachment issues. Secure attachment comes from having a stable base – damage should be avoided at all costs.

- From 18 months to three or four years old, children can handle less frequent visits than infants, but consistency and frequency are still very important. Visits of a lengthy duration are not recommended.

- With children under the age of three, the use of week-about arrangements is not in their best interests.

Visitation for other children

Prior to the year 2000, arrangements for children were relatively straightforward. The majority of children lived with their mother, who was typically the primary carer, and had every second weekend with their father. The rationale behind these arrangements was that the working father had limited availability. It was disruptive to the child to have contact with their father during school time, however free time was shared, so the father had half of the weekends and half of the holidays.

The advantage of these arrangements was that it maintained continuity for the children in the mother's household. Unfortunately, the significant disadvantage was the amount of contact with the father effectively ruled him out of being a significant part of the children's lives. The father became the 'Disney parent' who had the children for the good times but, because of the large gaps in contact, they did not establish a deep bond. Children and parents both missed out on a meaningful relationship. Often by the time teen years were under way the role of the father was discounted or forgotten.

In addition to the fact these arrangements were limited in their overall successfulness because of the watering down of the father's role, society has changed, which has been a significant factor. Men over the past 30 years have been seeking an increased role in the lives of their children, and women have in increasing numbers returned to the workforce, therefore the traditional family structure upon which that sort of arrangement was based has rapidly declined. As such, more children live in a situation where both parents have been, or are, in the workforce, or where there has been a reversal of roles in that the father stays at home and cares for the children (even today this occurs in a relatively minor percentage of households – e.g. men were the sole carers in less than 20 per cent of separated households in 2023).

Even prior to the changes in the legislation, the Family Court, and parents in general, had come to realise the fortnightly visitation arrangements were not in the children's best interests. The realisation was that children needed to develop a better relationship with their fathers. Therefore, for some time there has been an increased tendency for parents to have arrangements incorporating contact on every second weekend, with some regular contact on weekdays (e.g. one or two afternoons per week, which may or may not include overnight contact). This meant the father could be in the child's psychological world on a weekly basis at least.

The recent legislative changes are based on a supposition of shared care (sometimes called reasonable and meaningful time). The difficulty arises when translating this into an arrangement that is best for children. The fairest way of having shared care is a week-about arrangement (i.e. each parent has the child for one week at a time). However, there is no psychological evidence to show this is an arrangement which best serves the children. There are some children who find that type of arrangement beneficial. Typically, it is those children who either have a strong relationship with both parents and want to maintain the strong psychological bond with both parents, or are in a tension-filled situation and the children have chosen a week-about arrangement because it is perceived as 'fair' for the parents (and thus limits the conflict).

I have seen a number of children who report problems with the week-about arrangement. For example, *"I have two houses and no home"*, or *"Mum has a home, dad has a home, but I don't."* There are practical problems, such as children leaving important items like sports shoes in the wrong home (this can occur on a weekend or a weekday – the items cannot be left until later due to the length of time spent in each home). There are also emotional issues, such as the impact of different parenting routines and strategies.

There are several other ways of achieving a 50 per cent split which does not necessarily entail a week-about arrangement. This includes what the literature calls the 'Ackerman Plan', which sees one parent with the majority of school term contact and the other parent with the majority of holiday contact. Obviously, such an arrangement has some difficulties; first, whether the parent is available to take the holiday contact, and second, one parent has a larger proportion of the work and the other the recreational activities. However, it does allow the children to have a sense of stability in that they are in a regular place during school terms, and they have reasonably large blocks of contact with both parents.

If both parents do decide to adopt a 50 per cent shared arrangement, there is some literature that suggests other ways of dividing the time rather than on a week-about basis. One method which warrants consideration is based on blocks of two days followed by two blocks of five days, rather than blocks of seven days/seven days. This rotating pattern of two/two and five/five (2-2, 5-5) days does increase the number of transfers between the households, but it means the children have a higher frequency of contact with the parents.

It sounds complicated but in practice, the 2-2 5-5 model works like this: Monday and Tuesday with the father, Wednesday and Thursday with the mother, Friday to Tuesday with the father, and Wednesday to Sunday with the mother again. This ensures that each parent has both a weekend and weekdays. It keeps some of the weekdays the same for consistency with routines and activities. The period between visits with each parent is kept short. It fits parents who have regular part-time work and is great if a parent takes a child to an activity (e.g. dad is T-ball coach and T-ball is on Tuesdays). I can see considerable potential merit for younger children (for example, those under 10 years of age) and I am seeing it used in Australia with good results although there is limited research available.

When considering young children on an equal shared arrangement, a week is too long, while alternating nights is generally very unsettling. If such an arrangement is put in place for children four years and under, I would recommend considering a two day/two day/three-day split on an alternate week basis so the plan rotates between the parents. It takes some work to coordinate but allows the child to have frequent contact with both parents – but it is long enough for some stability? If that is not possible, three days/four days may be adequate.

From observation and feedback, parents who use the 2-2 5-5 plan find it works well, in particular for those who have similar parenting and good communication, and children who cope and are across the ages of 6 to 11. Once they get into early teens, the children often find it too disruptive changing house and then like longer blocks, like week-about or even fortnight-about.

I use the words "equal shared care" to describe arrangements of 50 per cent. The research also shows that if you have 30 to 35 per cent or more time you can end up with an equal relationship when the kids grow up to be adults. In other words, it does not have to be 50 per cent to build a solid relationship. It needs to be at least 30 per cent. Therefore, unequal shared care is possible. Unequal care has a primary base and visits to the other parent. This means that similarity of parenting and communication do not have to be as tight as is necessary for equal shared care.

The models of unequal shared-care arrangements include a ten/four, nine/five or eight/six split on a fortnightly basis. These are not equal sharing but allow both parents to have a meaningful involvement in the child's life. Once again, based on the literature, it is difficult to form a definitive opinion about the benefit of these arrangements. However, these models mirror attachment patterns that children start with a primary parent.

On the basis of my reading of the current literature, and experience with many children, I prefer that parents have an unequal shared-care model on either a nine day/five day or eight day/six-day arrangement when conflict is high and/or communication is low. This allows the child time for a good relationship with both parents but also allows for a primary base. In my opinion, for such an arrangement to work, the parents need to have a regular block of time (e.g. Thursday to Sunday night, which is four nights, and then in the following week have just the Thursday overnight). That way the period of time is never more than a week away from the visits. The child has a sense of a regular established household (i.e. the primary home) but gets good contact with the alternate parent. Both parents have some weekend and school time. This model works well if one parent is employed on a full-time basis.

If a nine day/five-day split is put in place it is important to talk to the children about how it is going. I saw two teenagers in one family who had this routine. Their arrangement was Thursday night one week, Thursday to Sunday nights the following week. The 15-year-old girl liked the regularity of this arrangement. She said the single night offered a great opportunity to *"download the issues of my week to dad"*. The 12-year-old boy who was not yet a teen wanted to shift the Thursday to the following week so he had the same amount of time but less changes of home during the week. He was also a child who kept leaving objects behind, such as musical and sporting equipment. He found the single night too much work for no major benefit.

Occasionally, parents come to me with alternate proposals, such as a fortnight or month-about arrangement. In my opinion these blocks of time are simply too long to make it viable for any children younger than teenage children who want the arrangement. A 14-year-old may cope quite well on a two-week cycle. How well the parents cope with lengthy gaps between visits is difficult to ascertain. With teenagers it may actually be a blessing!

I have even had parents propose contact in alternate years (i.e. one parent will be the primary parent one year with the other having regular contact, with the contact reversed in the alternate years). Quite apart from the various practical limitations with such an arrangement, I can find no particular psychological advantage to suggest this type of arrangement is appropriate.

It is important to note that often between 6 and 12 years of age unequal shared care often works well, but when children reach the teen years equal care is preferred. There can be less effective communication between the parents when children are teens as they can organise their own arrangements. Teens have some self-regulation and ability to deal with issues. Therefore, good co-parents consider changing the arrangements around the start of high school onwards depending on what the children want.

With any of these arrangements, the following factors have to be considered.

1. The employment arrangement of both parents. If the parents have shared care and place the child in day care or after-school care when the other parent is readily available, it seems to be a pointless exercise for the child's wellbeing. While good quality day care or after-school care has some advantages (e.g. mixing with other children) having an arrangement which denies contact with an available parent does not seem to make sense from a psychological point of view.

With respect to work, there are some parents who would be available for week-about arrangements, or who can take children to and from school, but unless there is a major restructuring of how Australian society views employment, the majority of people are going to struggle to fulfil such arrangements without using after-school care. In the case of public servants, it may be possible for them to have access to nine-day fortnights, in which case a nine day/five-day arrangement is viable.

2. Access to weekend time. Parents sometimes opt for a five day/two day split or four day/three day split where the working parent has each weekend. For example, I saw a nurse who works three regular weekend night shifts because the extra penalties meant she would earn in three days what normally takes her four shifts. This arrangement then effectively means the nurse only has the child during weekday time and does not have access to leisure activities. This may be effective for some parents but is often not practical for both parents.

3. Proximity of each parent. The closer parents live together the more viable shared care becomes. The proximity of parents to each other is particularly relevant as children get older so that they can have a social network. If the children go to school in one area and then spend their weekends in a different area, they become disadvantaged with respect to their social networks.

4. The greater the co-operation between the parents, the greater the flexibility. Children need to be able to go to sporting, cultural, religious, educational and social activities. I have assessed a number of cases where one

parent is not willing to take the child to parties during their weekends or enrol them in sport. I was involved in a case where each parent had the child enrolled in a different dance programme so the child had alternate weekends at different dance schools. These sorts of situations are just ludicrous and reflect parents engaged in personal power struggles with their children in the middle.

5. The views of the children, especially older children. The greater the opportunity for children to make decisions about their living arrangements the better. For example, I was involved in a case where the two parents lived in close proximity to each other. Their teenage child would ride his bike between the two homes. He had the flexibility to choose when he spent his time with which parent. He had one parent who was particularly good with mathematics, and the other parent who was particularly good with English. He used to spend most of his time with one parent, but would cycle to the other parent's house to stay on the nights he had maths homework.

6. Co-parenting issues. The greater the degree of co-operation, and the greater the similarity in parenting styles, the better the chance for shared-care arrangements to work. As stated earlier, co-parenting is really what is required for the children's best interests. Parallel parenting is a workable alternative but it does divide the care. However, if the styles involve remote control or crossover parenting, then shared care is not going to work. This leaves the alternative of defined visits on a more limited and traditional basis.

7. Lack of co-operation or conflict between parents. There is an argument in the literature that if parents are in conflict, then shared care is a way of helping the child to achieve a relationship with both parents. Some writers claim that conflict and a lack of co-operation does not prevent shared care. The evidence is not yet in. It may take another 10 years to conduct the research and have sufficient results to know definitively. However, from my experience, I would suggest that if parents have intense conflict, but can parallel parent, then an unequal shared-care arrangement may help a child to have a relationship with both parents. Some children in conflict want the arrangements to be week-about as it is "fair" and avoids them having to take sides. However, if the child is subject to crossover parenting styles, especially coupled with intense family conflict, then any type of shared care is likely to keep the child in a constant state of tension (and in my opinion likely to be detrimental to their psychological wellbeing). Similarly, if the conflict between the parents involves the children, then shared care is likely to damage the children rather than diffuse the issues.

8. Children with special issues. Some children are suited to shared arrangements, while others may not cope. Children with conditions like attention deficit disorder will do best with the parent who has the strictest routines (see the section on neuro-developmental conditions). The children should be in one place during the school week. Children with conditions such as developmental delays, autism and anxiety disorders, in particular, will not cope with changing routines and will probably

do best in a single household but it depends on the individual child..

9. Monitoring the children. Parents should monitor their children to see if they are coping, and if they like a shared arrangement. Between the ages of 6 and 12 one arrangement may work, but as children hit their teens they often want to stay in one home. One child may like the time between parents to be short because they like the relationship with their parents, others may prefer the longer blocks so they do not have to change houses so often.

A final point I would like to make is that in the Western world children have a lot of holidays, around three months in total. In my opinion time with children during holidays builds relationships while term time is maintenance. When you think about your childhood do you remember the parent who made your lunch and got you to school, or do you remember the holidays and recreational activities with fond memories? For most people it is the build which comes from holiday adventures. Therefore, ensuring you have good quality holiday time and you are available to take it, should be a priority. Term time is nice but whether it is equal or unequal will have less impact in the long-term relationship. However, not having holiday time will make a significant impact on the future quality of your relationship with that child.

Key Points

- The legislative changes propose shared care, preferably equal care, for separating couples. The fairest way of achieving shared care is a week-about arrangement (i.e. each parent has the child for one week at a time) or a similar arrangement. However, there is no psychological evidence to show this is an arrangement which best serves the children.

- There are some children who find a shared-care arrangement beneficial. If the children have a strong relationship with both parents, or are in a tension-filled situation, the children may choose a week-about arrangement because it is perceived as 'fair' for the parents (and thus limits the conflict).

- There are many children who report problems with the week-about arrangements. These include a lack of a sense of home, always packing, leaving things behind, and the impact of different parenting routines.

- Equal time can be achieved in a variety of ways. One parent can have more term time and the other more holiday time, or alternative schedules can be considered (such as two days, two days, then five days, five days).

- Shared-care arrangements do not have to be equal time. Other arrangements may be better for children, including options such as a ten/four, nine/five or eight/six split on a fortnightly basis. While these arrangements are not sharing on an equal basis, they allow both parents to have a meaningful involvement in the child's life while giving the child a home base.

- Whichever arrangement is put in place it is important to review it with the children. They may want different arrangements as they get older.

- Very few younger children like arrangements involving alternating blocks of fortnightly or monthly periods. These blocks of time are simply too long for most children below the age of 12.
- When considering arrangements for the children the following practical issues need to be kept in mind:
  - Work schedules of both parents
  - Access to weekend and weekday time without being too disruptive to routines
  - Proximity of houses
  - The degree of co-operation
  - Views of the children
  - The amount of conflict
  - Special needs of children
  - Ability of the children to cope.
  - A final observation I have made is that term time is maintenance, while holiday time builds relationships. Make sure you have quality holiday time and use it well.

Nesting

Jokingly, I once said to a barrister that what is best for children is they stay in the home and the parents move in and out. A short while later, I read some literature which discussed this as a shared-care technique, using the term 'nesting'. In other words, the children stay in the nest and the parents rotate through it.

This sort of arrangement may be viable for a short period of time, however, as a longer-term solution it is fraught with problems. If the children are very small and the parties are working out finances to enable another house to be purchased, nesting can be very helpful. I mentioned earlier that sameness is a good way to help children cope with change. Staying in the same house with the same parents, albeit one at a time gives a lot of sameness. Their life is good.

However, the problems from nesting are complex. The first issue is trust. One parent leaves the home, and the other parent moves in. Everything from the email directory to the refrigerator can become a possible concern (e.g. reading private information or using the other parent's shopping). It may be that rooms have to be locked or be off limits. This can get complicated. In some of the more sinister cases I have had parents using the baby monitor connected to the internet to spy on what is happening.

Assuming the couple can sort out those arrangements and they can treat each other with respect, the next obstacle comes into play when someone re-partners. This can create a whole set of strange relationship cycles. Does the new partner come into the house with the parent? If they have children, do the children come as well? Do they sleep in the former marital bed? Who changes the sheets? These and other such questions must be considered at a practical level.

I am firmly of the opinion that nesting is only a solution while parents sort out other arrangements, or to start overnight visitations with a baby or infant. Nesting may be a preferred option for parents who live in an acrimonious situation, have not been able to work out a regime for the children or are waiting for a trial. However, in the long term, separation requires the parents disengage from each other and start their own lives. Nesting keeps them in a holding pattern and does not allow them to start building their own new life. Psychologically, it is essential for good mental health that each parent has a new life. Obviously, the initiator will be ready for this sooner than the non-initiator. Nonetheless, the non-initiator has to work through their emotions, and this can only take place once they are free to do so.

I was involved in a case where the parents shared the former matrimonial home for over a year post-separation, the father living upstairs and the mother living downstairs. The children were living in what I described in the report as a 'cold war'. There was ongoing and intense tension in the home and, although the parents spoke to each other in a civil manner, the children felt the underlying tension. However, the parents could not sort out the living arrangements for the children (which was also linked to the final property settlement). Hence, they were in limbo pending a trial. This would have been a case where a 'nesting' arrangement may have helped to take some of the pressure off the children pending the settlement of the issues but in the process kept everyone in a state of tension.

It should be clear by now that I am not a fan of nesting arrangements. However, they have a place and are an important arrangement to consider in certain circumstances. They do not make good final arrangements.

Key points

- Nesting may be a possible short-term strategy for co-operative parents to provide stability to the children while practical issues are resolved.

- Nesting can be useful in establishing a relationship with a baby or infant as the child stays in a familiar environment.

- Nesting is not an effective long-term solution due to issues related to adults commencing new lives.

Children Who Refuse Contact

At the start of this book, I described how early in my career I assessed a family of eight – a mother, father and six children. When I interviewed the children and asked what they called their father, they said "Thing". The three oldest children elaborated by saying that on a Friday night the three of them stayed up later than usual with their mum, they ate pizza, watched a movie together, and celebrated no "thing" in the house. All of the children were refusing to see the father. All of the children were doing well in life – the usual parameters such as school performance, general emotional presentation – except for this attitude towards their father. I did not have an answer to the case back then, and 35 years later there are multiple different views in the literature but still no standardised answer on how to deal with cases like this.

I also had an experience where I assessed a family, and the dynamic within that family confirmed there was a substantial problem. I recommended the mother have majority care otherwise I predicted the child, when he was a teenager, would be aligned with dad and not be seeing mum. Eventually, my office got a phone call from the distressed mother saying she had not seen her son for nine months and the son was now living with the father. He had recently turned 14. When I wrote the initial report, he was just 2½. The psychological dynamics leading to that outcome were clearly evident 12 years before the eventual outcome.

Earlier I proffered the view there are only five strategies children have with which to cope when they are in a conflict. Some children can tell it how it is, but most of the time children are told by parents what to do and how to function. A number of children find ways to duck beneath the conflict. There are essentially two ways of doing this: they can tell parents what they want the parents to hear, or they can tell the parents nothing. A fourth position is to take sides. The fifth type of coping which I have observed in a small number of children who have an equally strong attachment to both parents is to trust neither. The parents are telling them different things, resulting in children who cannot decide which parent they want to believe. These children end up not trusting anybody. It is the taking of sides which I would like to particularly address.

There are several factors which shape the choices of children when they are in a conflict. These have been touched on earlier but I will reiterate them here for the purpose of this chapter.

1. Their stage of development is important. For example, it is quite common that children 12 and above take sides to get out of the conflict because they are beginning to get some of their own independence and ability to express opinions.

2. The way in which the parents deal with the children, in my opinion, is a large motivation. For children the fear of the loss of the love of the preferred parent is strong.

Loss of love is an incredibly powerful motivator to do what the parent wants.

3. It is influenced by the child's level of understanding. I note there is a disproportionate number of children taking sides who have ADHD, learning difficulties, autism and so on, and the common feature is these children are all more black and white in their thinking, which makes it easier for them to take a side, as one parent is right, one is wrong. They cannot tolerate ambiguity.

4. In every family we talk about expressions such as "daddy's girl" or "mummy's boy". Children have natural connections easier with one parent than the other. Some parents work away, some parents are present but emotionally absent, and so forth. All of this shapes the pre-existing relationships the child may have. Obviously, it is easier for a child to align with the parent they feel strongest to, although a small number of children will align in the opposite direction for fear of losing the other parent.

5. One of the other factors is grief, and grieving the loss of a parent, the break-up and so forth, takes its toll on children.

The key point I would stress is, in the current climate, a very common allegation is, "She is alienating the children from me" meaning the other parent is not seeing the child. The word alienation is a controversial term. Some professionals will not use it at all, other people use it in a particular way.

Nicholas Bala is a writer in the family law space who produced this most useful model which shows the post-separation possibilities for children which include:

- Strong attachment to both parents.
- An affinity to one parent but attached to both.
- Aligning with one parent but still having contact with the other parent.
- Justified rejection where a child does not have a connection or has a reason to not like a parent (for example a history of abuse).
- Alienation where a child who previously had a strong relationship with that parent is now rejecting that parent for no apparent substantial reason.

The key to understanding the situation is that it is not about *what* the children are doing, but *why* they are doing it. Forcing a child to see a partner when they have a justified rejection is likely to be harmful, whereas a child who is aligning may well be harmed if it is not forced.

A common argument in the literature is that parents who do this are personality disordered. Certainly, some personality-disordered parents do this, but my observation is the only area where some of these parents show personality-disordered behaviour is in regard to their ex-partner and at no other point of their life, not even in their early developmental history. There is often a common group where there are some highly anxious parents, there are some who are mentally ill, there is also some interesting research on the concept of moral disengagement. The essence of the research comes from a Spanish study looking at moral disengagement versus what is known as "The dark triad" personality factors (Clemente, Espinosa & Padilla, 2019). The dark triad meaning that they have traits of Machiavellianism, narcissism and psychopathy. Moral disengagement is a psychological process where parents override their normal moral code for a particular purpose. The result showed moral disengagement appeared to be a significantly stronger predictor of the willingness to harm a partner in a custody dispute than the dark triad variables. While this is early days in the research, it actually made sense to me. What we need to do is work out a bit more about what causes people to override their moral code.

Alienation becomes a type of moral disengagement. In the process of moral disengagement, the parent feels morally justified and then uses the belief to distort the children's own moral justification. In the process, they will use the following:

- Denigration. The parent indicates that: *"I'm better, I know how to look after you, he was never there, he was abusive."*

- They create an absence of guilt. There is a reward rather than punishment for negative behaviour to do with the other parent.

- Reinforce scenarios that are negative as proof, for example, *"Daddy hurt me when I was in mummy's tummy"*. This is something the child would not otherwise even be aware of.

- Dehumanising. Have derogatory names (e.g. "thing").

- Induce fear in the child: *"If you see them, you'll never come home"*; *"You will lose my love"*, or *"They may steal you"*.

This was how I was able to pick the parent with the two-year-old and predict it was likely to become an alienation case when the child was older because these types of moral disengagement factors were evident in the parent.

This leads me to reinforce the first key point about allegations of alienation and that is that children's behaviour often superficially looks as if they do not want to see the other parent, but we have to dig deep to find out why they are doing what they are doing.

This, then, leads to a change of residence as an option (discussed in detail in the next section) which should be considered. If a parent is morally corrupting a child, it should be relatively straightforward to recognise they should be removed, for example, if the court is convinced they are making false allegations of sexual abuse, the child has been led to believe false aspects and, as such, is being morally corrupted. A definitive finding is not always possible as the evidence is not always clear.

One of the arguments for changing residence of a child who is refusing contact is to enable them to have a relationship with both parents. Unfortunately, this is not always the case. Removing a child from one parent may end up with the child being with that parent and not seeing the first parent and, other than creating a disruption in the child's life, the child is no better off with the second parent than the first.

Some jurisdictions remove children quickly and commonly in these types of cases, others do it rarely. The jurisdiction I practise in does it relatively rarely. It is interesting to observe and follow up some of the cases.

One of my arguments has been that there needs to be a solid, pre-existing attachment to make it work. However, I was involved in a case where contact had been stopped for several years and, before then, dad had only ever had every second weekend. The court was convinced the mother was creating false sexual abuse allegations and moved the two children from mum to dad. Mum was subject to a period of 90 days of no time with the children until she had completed certain courses. She did not engage in the courses, and I was then asked to do a reassessment when the teenage girl became suicidal and wanted to see mum. This girl coped extremely badly. However, the older brother was perfectly happy living with dad, was willing to see mum but had no thought or fantasy about living with mum and preferred to stay with dad.

It begs the question, why are the two children reacting differently? It goes back to the reality that there are multiple factors which shape what happens to children, including pre-existing relationships, the personalities of the children and the dynamics leading to the situation. It is critical the court and parents understand there is no one-size-fits-all.

The problematic behaviour of the parent often continues. For example, in one long-term case the child was eventually placed with dad, and it reached the point where mum had a no contact order. Mum had gone to court to try to resume contact, but over that period it was found the child had a mobile phone hidden in a neighbour's letterbox and was picking-up the phone on the way to school and putting it back after school. The child accidentally put it in the wrong letterbox, and it was found. On the phone were text messages from mum advising the child to make up sexual abuse allegations about her father, all this while she is trying to legally regain contact.

I think it is critical all workers in this area understand that individual psychological therapy with an alienating parent will not work, particularly if the person is not experienced in Family Court dynamics. They tend to cause an alignment with the parent and reinforce the parent's belief. The interventions which work require quite a directive approach, and parents need to be made accountable for what behaviours are appropriate and inappropriate. Therefore, some types of directive family therapy may help swing medium-based cases. In the more extreme cases, ultimately, change of residence may be an option but, hopefully, I have highlighted the point that it is not a simple option, it does not work for all children, and even children within the same family may have a very different experience of what has just happened to them.

Key Points

- Resisting and refusing contact with the other parent is a topic fraught with issues making it difficult to understand and is one of the most complex and least understood areas of family dynamics.

- Children can have strong attachment to both parents; an affinity to one parent but attached to both; aligning with one parent but still having contact with the other parent; justified rejection where a child does not have a connection or has a reason to not like a parent; or alienation where a child who has previously had a strong relationship with that parent is now rejecting that parent for no apparent substantial reason.

- The key to understanding the refusal is it is not about *what* the children are doing, but *why* they are doing it.

- Solutions are complex – forcing a child to see a partner when they have a justified rejection is likely to be harmful, whereas a child who is aligning may well be harmed if they are not forced to see the other parent.

The Case for No Contact or Change of Residence

On separation there are sometimes arguments that one parent should have no contact with the children. These sorts of cases typically involve allegations of sexual abuse, alienation or family violence.

As a Single Expert in Family Court cases, there have been occasions where it has been necessary to recommend a no-contact arrangement. Basically, these are cases where the level of risk to the children's physical and/or psychological wellbeing is unacceptably high and this risk cannot be managed. Sometimes there is also a risk to the safety or wellbeing of the other parent.

In my opinion, children who may have been involved in family violence situations or in other forms of abuse, do best if they learn to safely face the abusive parent rather than simply avoid any relationship whatsoever. This view is not shared by some of my colleagues, and we would therefore differ in relation to the level of abuse that we consider would constitute an unacceptable risk, and whether contact should take place. However, the basic question to be addressed is whether there is scope to minimise harm and gain positive benefits. The essence of my argument is if you face the fear, you lose the fear, if not the fear remains active. Therefore, a child may picture someone who is abusive as a source of fear until they actually see them. When they safely see them, they can learn it is just another person who was behaving badly.

I note some family violence perpetrators, especially those engaged in coercive control, use court as another way of controlling the victim. These people never want to stop the relationship and, if properly identified, should be thwarted in their quest against the victim. The tricky thing is they are often good at playing the victim and look like they are hard done by.

Some years ago I was made aware of children who were the product of IVF donation who sought to change the privacy law to enable them to contact their sperm donor fathers. The original law prevented them from knowing their donor fathers. Some of these children had grown up in healthy functioning families, but still had a strong desire to understand their biological heritage. Similarly, adoption has almost disappeared around the world as the concept of integrating a child into a new family was found to be a flawed logic. Therefore, there appears to be a drive for people to understand where they have come from and to seek out that information. In a no-contact situation the child would not have access to the information to answer some of these questions. Establishing an avenue of contact would make sense to enable such issues to be addressed.

As discussed earlier, a final reason why I generally avoid proposing a no-contact arrangement relates to the difference between the real and imagined parent. We all have an ideal of what a father and mother should be. If we do not have contact with a parent, with all of their flaws and problems, then we can only rely on the fantasy image of that parent. Psychologically, in the long-term, children will be better off knowing what their father or mother is really like, even if some of this is negative. They can learn to manage the problems and not create a fantasy. However, I must stress that with any of these arrangements it is very important to ensure the child is kept safe.

Cases in which I have recommended no contact include that of a father who, after separation, had physically and sexually assaulted the mother in a violent fashion, was subsequently jailed and then repeated the offence while on parole. It was evident the level of impulsivity was beyond a manageable level and the amount of time involved in the incidents meant this person had an ongoing preoccupation. A second case involved a father who had been jailed for sexually assaulting his stepson, and who was seeking to have contact with his biological children. He had been able to seriously sexually abuse the stepson over a period of several years without the child disclosing it. A father such as this had a tremendous capacity to manipulate and, although he had not harmed his biological children, the impact within the family was too great to allow the recommendation of any form of contact. A third example concerned a man with a significant intellectual disability and behavioural problems who wanted to have contact with his son (who also had an intellectual disability). The boy had not seen his father for three years. In that case, the child did not have the capacity to understand the relationship and the father lacked the capacity to act appropriately or safely.

A different type of example was a case where it was deemed sexual abuse did not happen but the mother continued to have the child believe they were abused. The court was of the view that child was being harmed by having this false belief. We know when children believe abuse to be real, they will show symptoms as if it was real. This means that a change of

Shared Care and Other Options

residence needs to happen, and it may result in the child not having contact with the parent. Removal from a prime parent is complex in its impact.

My position for cases such as the last one is if the court is to remove the children from the prime caring parent, they need to use it wisely. This is where mental health practitioners doing the assessment need to be careful, lawyers need to ensure the evidence is clear, and the judge must be satisfied it is the least damaging path. I definitely do not think removal should be a first resort, but it should also not be a last resort. There needs to be clear evidence of serious psychological harm by that parent, such as a child believing false allegations. It is important to remember there is no such thing as neutral behaviour, everything has an impact. Removal will be a major rupture in the child's life, so is it the least damaging pathway? We know it is going to work better if there were good pre-existing relationships with the parent who is not having contact rather than a previously absent parent. And it should never be used if the child is aligning based on justified fears or a lack of compatibility between the parent and the child. Recent alignments are easier to change than longstanding problems.

If the child is seeing both parents, or is capable of seeing both parents, that should be explored before changing residence. With younger children the attachment needs to be considered, so sometimes an interim arrangement should be implemented where time is gradually increased to equal time. This allows the court the option of change of residence should the problems continue, and the behaviours not change.

In summary there are no simple solutions to complex family problems. Removing a parent from the life of child has implications in the short, medium and long term. It is important to remember the child is half of each parent biologically, and it is hard to have a healthy identity if half of your heritage and disposition is so bad that you should never see them. It is essential all these implications are properly considered first because the short-term gain by lowering some issues leaves a long-term gap.

Key Points

- In cases of domestic violence or child abuse, the basic question to be addressed is whether there is scope to minimise harm and gain positive benefits. The safety of the child must be paramount.

- Psychologically, in the long term, children will be better off knowing what their father or mother is really like, even if some of this is negative. This is best achieved by the child having small but safely administered doses of reality.

- Where barring a parent from being in the life of a child is considered, it is critical that the short, medium and long-term implications are carefully considered.

- Change of residence needs to be considered carefully before being applied. It should not be a first-line strategy nor should it be a case of last resort.

Substance Abuse and Addiction

A common situation leading to separation is that of a partner who has a significant drug or alcohol problem which has not been addressed. Drugs such as amphetamines, cocaine or heroin have significant psychological effects on the ability of a person to care for a child, as does chronic alcohol abuse. If a parent has a substantial problem and cannot control their use, then contact may need to be either supervised or extremely limited. Such drug use usually means the person is not available on a psychological level. Actively seeking the drug may mean children are left alone or dodgy characters are coming to the home. Neglect may be a problem, and stimulant drugs may increase violence to extremely dangerous levels.

In this day and age occasional marijuana smoking is relatively common in the community, however, in my opinion, chronic marijuana smoking has significant impacts on parenting. It may be at a level where parenting arrangements need to be quite limited. Not only does it impact on motivation, short-term memory and mood, it can also trigger paranoia or depression. It is not a harmless drug, especially when taken on a chronic basis.

The abuse of prescription medication can have serious ramifications for a family. Often the drugs are of sedative or anti-anxiety nature (codeine, oxycodone, Valium and other benzodiazepines). These types of drugs lower awareness, make people sleepy, and if mixed with alcohol can have complex reactions. Heavy use can be problematic, especially if people are self-medicating excessively.

People with substance abuse problems and who are stabilised on medications which are used to treat addiction (such as methadone for heroin) may or may not be able to parent, depending on the circumstance, medication dosage and adjunct treatment regimes. Drug counsellors often recommend the recovering parent have the child as an aid to recovery. However, if you read that last statement carefully, you will understand the contact is for the benefit of the parent – not the child! I appreciate it may help the mental health of someone in recovery to have their children, but it is the child we must prioritise.

Even properly prescribed medications, such as sleeping tablets and tranquillisers can affect parenting by slowing the parent's responses (e.g. not waking when a child has a problem in the night). In light of my earlier comments that depression is a common occurrence at the time of break-up, people are therefore more likely to use medications to help with depression and sleep disturbances during the first year or two post-separation. It is important to be careful when using these medications if you are the sole parent in the house.

In addition, it is of concern that alcohol and marijuana are often used to self-medicate depression. It is important that parents, especially men, take care not to create additional problems for themselves and the children by using intoxicating substances and, because emotions have been inhibited, doing something stupid.

Another type of addiction is electronic. People use online games, chat, gambling (both online or in real time) and pornography to escape the realities of their life. Excessive engagement of these things can lead to sleep deprivation and preoccupation with their activity online rather than parenting their children. The direct risk between viewing adult pornography and child related offending may be low but children may still be exposed to images and adult sexual contact they should not see. Child porn users also have a low rate of committing real time offences, but specialist opinion is required around risk when there is evidence of child porn viewing.

Common to all addiction is that the person is using a "thing" to address their issues. Healthy functioning people need to turn to people to resolve their issues, not things. Things do not resolve problems. If someone has had an addiction, suddenly ceasing it does not mean they are cured. Relapse is common in all addictions (around two-thirds relapse within 12 months and in some studies those with heavy addictions have a 90 per cent relapse rate). Caution in regards to time with the children is necessary for the first 12 months of ceasing the addiction, and even the second year is a risk period. Generally, it is considered to be two years for someone to be classed as in remission.

Curing an addiction often requires digging deep into early attachment issues and trauma experienced. Therefore, good therapy is necessary to help someone with an addiction get better. Without it they may simply turn to another type of addiction. Most addicts have comorbid conditions (drugs, gambling, porn etc.) rather than just one. Ceasing the behaviour does not mean they have addressed the emotional drivers. There is also an argument that addictions cannot be cured, only managed.

Key Points

- Substance abuse impacts on parenting. Serious drug problems need to be addressed, and while being addressed, time with the children may need to be limited or supervised.

- Chronic marijuana smoking and alcohol intoxication impact on parenting in significant ways. Children need parents who are emotionally and practically available to them.

- It is important sole parents ensure that even prescription medication does not interfere with parenting capacity.

- Stopping an addictive behaviour does not mean that a person is cured. It means they have stopped but the dynamic may still be present, unless work is done to address the emotional causes of the addictive behaviour. Cure of addiction requires digging deep into early attachment issues and trauma experienced.

Separating Siblings

When there are several siblings in a family the issue of separating the children sometimes is raised as an option. Some parents propose that, in the case of two children, one child goes with each parent. This often occurs when the children are viewed as property rather than as people. Generally speaking, children should be kept together. When parents have long ceased to exist, the sibling bond will continue.

There are some children who simply do not get on with each other. However, the research on sibling rivalry often shows that parental favouritism has created that rivalry. If two children are of similar ages and do not get on, then examining how each parent relates to the children will be important when addressing the problem. Separating the children may actually make the situation worse in that they see the separation as either further favouritism or rejection.

Post separation, people re-partner. Sometimes they rush into situations which do not last. Having formed a blended family which has not worked out, the situation becomes complicated – children together in a house do not have step or half siblings, they are all brothers and sisters. The issue of stepchildren maintaining contact after separation is significant. Generally speaking, I believe the psychological relationship between people is a more significant factor than biology. Therefore, ongoing contact after separation when the blended family does not work is beneficial for the children but can be difficult to ensure. However, this becomes complicated when the parents re-partner again. For example, there may be a biological father, a stepfather, followed by a new partner on the scene. Ideally, it is better to allow time to fade step-sibling and step-parent relationships than to terminate them suddenly.

The separation of siblings may arise in those rare cases where there is a significant age difference between the children. An older child may have a particular wish to be with one parent whereas a younger child may be better placed with the other parent. This alone would not be a reason to separate them, but the larger the age difference the more the children may be considered in their own light. For example, a 16-year-old boy and his 11-year-old sister are unlikely to have much overlap in their psychological worlds at this stage. However, when the boy is 26 years old and his sister is 21 they may have a greater commonality of interest. If they had been separated earlier there would be limited chance for this commonality.

In the rare cases where siblings are to be separated, it is important to ensure the arrangement allows for frequent contact between the children. For example, in a case in which I had to make recommendations in relation to a 15-year-old boy and a

10-year-old girl, I offered the following – the 15-year-old boy chose to live with his father, so I recommended this take place. The 10-year-old girl was living on a week-about basis with both parents, so I recommended that the arrangement continue. I then proposed the 15-year-old boy visit his mother for four days a fortnight. This meant that, although the children were legally separated, they were actually apart from each other for only three days per fortnight (the four days the boy spent with his mother was during the same week the girl lived with the mother).

In some of the complex resist-and-refuse cases, children may be with a parent and not have time with the other parent. I cited a case earlier where there were three children, one with mum not seeing dad, one with dad not seeing mum, and one going between the two. At the end of the day this was happening as nothing else was possible. It was not because it was the best outcome for the children. They should have been seeing both parents.

Occasionally, I have seen a family where there are special needs children who have very demanding health or psychological needs. Sometimes they require an excessive amount of care, other times them may be volatile and dangerous. In a few cases the necessary outcome has been to separate these children. When this happens, it is important the siblings still maintain time.

Key Points

- As a general rule, siblings should not be separated.

- Even if there may appear to be no short-term benefits in children staying together because of differences of age and interest, once they become adults the situation may be different.

- Blended families are complicated in that there will be step and half-siblings who have well-established relationships. Careful consideration needs to be given to the needs of all children after separation.

- Parents need to choose partners wisely and introduce them to children carefully as there are complications if it does not work out.

- Ideally, it is better to allow time to fade step-sibling and step-parent relationships than to terminate them suddenly.

6

Final Words

Strive to Thrive

A lawyer and I wrote a brief summary guide called "Strive to Thrive". It is essentially a summary of what *Shared Care and Divided Lives* is trying to tell you and I am reproducing a select and modified portion of it here as it has the essential co-parenting elements in a nutshell. This is my last effort at trying to prime your focus on actions which will result in having mentally healthy children after separation.

A court can order time but it cannot order parents to be reasonable. It is up to you and your ex-partner to do that. You have to remember they are your ex-partner but they are never the ex-parent of the children. Your rejected partner is the only other real parent your children will ever have. Children do not need to feel their loved parent is a reject. The key points being to model good behaviour and striving to give your children the best co-parenting they can have.

Raising children is now your business. You do not have to like your business partner – you only have to value the product. Your product is successful, well-adjusted children who become amazing adults. Do everything you can to achieve that goal. The first step is to press reset on the relationship you used to have and start the build as business partners.

Work hard to communicate in the way you would want to be spoken to by your ex-partner. Use the model of communication by Bill Eddy called BIFF (Brief, Informative, Firm, Friendly). Reminder it contains no *"I feel"* or *"you are"* – these two expressions should be banned from your communication. Make sure you are using this business model to express what the children need.

Children will do what it takes to survive so you need to ensure they thrive not just survive. Work hard to compromise and negotiate parenting styles and routines so the children do not have to lead two different lives as two different people. Do this by outlining in your communication the advantages of why you think it is good for the children. An ex-partner may not care what you want but will often listen to what is best for the children. If you end up in different parenting worlds, the children will have to go into survival mode rather than thriving.

Work hard to keep children completely out of the separation in every way possible. I believe children should have layers for truth. They need to know what is going on but at age-appropriate levels. Saying things are "adult business" is very protective but they still need some information to not be anxious. Give them what they need to know in a way which makes them less anxious.

Children need two homes and not two houses. Work hard at showing your children that while they live in two places, their lives will not be split in two, they will have two parents at sporting, life and school events. The more seamless the transitions, the more normal their life will be.

Work hard to communicate respectfully, to act and speak about the other parent respectfully, to find a parenting arrangement that helps the children. It is important to realise you can only be responsible for your half of the co-parenting situation. You need to conduct yourself with dignity and honour. Did you know children notice who smiles at handover? They also notice who does not! However, one day your children will be adults and they will look back and judge you on what you have done, and they will remember. Truth floats with time, and research shows children will be closest to the parents they thought were fairest. In other words, model good behaviour as your children are recording your every actions.

Work hard to ensure your children are not a message-relay service to convey messages to the other parents, leaving them wondering why a kid has to do something their own parents cannot. There are plenty of excellent applications to aid communication, start with co-parenting apps OurFamilyWizard, and 2houses to see what these can do.

Ensure children are never put in a position they must keep information from the other parent, whether that be a sleepover at a friend's house, a new mobile phone or medical/therapeutic treatment they are receiving. Parents would never tell children it is acceptable to keep secrets from them, so why would it ever be okay to encourage, support, condone or even worse, tell their children to keep secrets from their other parent?

Love is something which builds not diminishes with quantity. Above all, remember it is okay for your child to love both parents, have a good time with both parents and be loved by both parents. You also cannot have too many people love your children, so let the family and friends on both sides add to the depth of the quality of the life your children are getting.

The expression, it takes a village to raise a child, is as relevant today as it ever was. In this context, it is important for both parents to bring their personal village to provide good quality parenting. This would include both parents, grandparents, aunts, uncles, cousins and friends. This is for both parents' respective sides of the family. It is also important you help your village to support co-parenting rather than tribal warfare. A grandparent, aunty or uncle can do a lot of damage to the children if you do not help manage your personal village.

Parents should also consider the benefit of having a professional village if the break-up is complex. This may vary from time to time depending on circumstances and needs, but could include a family lawyer, a family dispute resolution practitioner, a regular GP and a treating psychologist/counsellor. Parents can also access support services and courses from organisations who support families and children and promote and teach skills to help parents provide good quality parenting to their children. Please note that the professional village for the children will be more beneficial if both homes use the same services such as the same GP and child psychologist. You may need your own village for your own professional needs.

If all else fails, remember the expression I gave earlier – love your children more than you hate your ex-partner. Always put children before conflict, not just through words but with actions.

Key Points

- You have an ex-partner but the children should never have an ex-parent.

- Do you want your children to thrive in life, or just survive? The power to change this is in the hands of the parents.

- Your future is a business of raising amazing children, so press reset, do not let the old relationship get in the way of your children's future.

- Work hard to communicate in the way you would want to be spoken to. Reminder to ban the words *"I feel"* or *"you are"*, it is now all about BIFF (Brief, Informative, Firm and Friendly).

- Children need two homes, not two houses.

- You cannot have too many people love your children.

- Control your village, the children do not need tribal warfare.

- Love your children more than you hate your ex-partner – put children before conflict – always.

Conclusion

Hopefully at this point you have gained a sense of the profound complexity of the issues for children in separation. Children's individual personality differences, their developmental stages and pre-existing attachment patterns have a large impact on how they will cope with separation. However, the actions of the parents will have the biggest impact on how children cope. Parents must sort out their emotional issues and deal with their own stage of grief if they are to minimise the effects on the children.

Within this mix of psychology, biology, emotion and attitude are the children of separated parents. By almost every known psychological measure, children of parental break-up are worse off in the short and long-term when compared to children raised in functional homes. Nothing can compensate for the loss of the advantage of having two parents functioning effectively in one home. Children in a family that functions fairly poorly are often still better off with two parents than one. Unless the situation is significantly abusive, the damage from separation is hard to overcome. The fact of critical importance is that the greater the conflict post-separation, the worst the outcome for the children.

From the child's perspective I would say to parents, if it is at all possible, stay together. While this may seem strange in a book about living arrangements for children of parental separation, if you want what is best for the children, consider whether the situation is fixable. Is the relationship truly over, or are you telling yourself this to justify your actions? Get some serious help and fix your problems. Your kids want and need both parents in the home and, even 10 years from separation, over half of all children will still fantasise about their parents getting back together. However, it is important you do not stay if you and the children are at risk of harm and that harm cannot be mitigated.

If you are a lawyer, before committing your client to serious adversarial action, ensure this is the only path for them. While a lawyer has a duty of care to represent their client's interest, I believe we all have a social duty in relation to the wellbeing of children. It is important this factor is canvassed prior to engaging in actions which may irreparably seal the fate of the relationship and the future of the children. Once that first lawyer letter is sent, there is no going back to trying to negotiate an outcome – the declaration of war has been made.

Assuming the only course of action is separation, there is no single living arrangement applicable to all families and circumstances. The key aspect is for children to have a meaningful long-term relationship with both their mother and father if they are to become their best selves. This is where establishing the best care arrangement becomes paramount. By best care I am referring to working through all the different factors for your own unique parenting arrangement. Under the Australian Family Court system, parenting plans need to be developed. The purpose of this book is to help you consider the issues about what is best for children so you can develop a plan which will be meaningful and effective – a best care plan.

A particular issue of concern is the importance of establishing a shared-care arrangement where the best interests of the children are shared between two parents. Although from a parent's point of view a shared arrangement is half the time, from a child's point of view a shared arrangement is where both parents have an active and meaningful involvement in the child's life. The only children who count the number of days with each parent to see if they are equal are ones who are drawn into their parents' dramas. Most children adapt to reasonably predictable arrangements. In this book I have tried to provide explanations of the various factors a parent can choose when establishing a shared-care arrangement. As stated earlier, I have a preference for arrangements which preserve a home base but where the child has solid time with the other parent (e.g. nine day/five day shared care for primary school aged children). However, this varies on a case-by-case basis depending on the facts.

The alternatives to a shared arrangement are the child either misses out on the input of both parents because one of them has insufficient time in the child's life to make a meaningful difference or has a divided life. The divided life occurs when the parents are so set in their ways that their lack of agreement and other problems (which probably led to the separation in the first place) result in the child having to go between two separate worlds. The child is living a divided life – they are not in shared care.

The choices are sharing the life, dividing the life, or not being involved in the life. Only shared care is going to truly benefit the child. Whether considering these issues from the perspective of a parent, or a worker within the legal arena, it is important we do not kid ourselves that we have established a shared-care arrangement when all we have effectively done is divided the child's life into equal or near equal sections of time. It is critical for a child's adjustment that the care is truly shared. Co-parenting is about being able to co-operate with the other parent to make time work.

In the professional literature some of the books about child custody evaluation begin with the Old Testament story of King Solomon. The story of King Solomon is about a judgement King Solomon has to make involving two women with competing claims over a child. The story begins with two women living together in the same house, each giving birth to a child. Sadly, one of the children dies. Both claim the remaining child to be their living son. They approach King Solomon to decide what should happen with the remaining child. King Solomon draws a sword and asks that the child be brought forth so that he can cut the child in half – one half for each woman. One woman exclaimed, *"Oh my Lord, give her the living child and in no way slay it."* The other said, *"It shall be neither mine nor thine. Divide it."* King Solomon answered and said, *"Give the child to the first woman who was prepared to let the child live at any cost."*

The healthy parent does not seek their half of the child, but seeks that the child may live at any cost. Separation is one of the most difficult experiences for both parents and children, and it is absolutely critical the child is given the best chance to live a full life. The above discussion does not provide a simple plan or structure to follow but it does provide some ideas to consider seriously. When reflecting on the material provided here, I would like to stress that I understand you are going through the most difficult time of your life, and it is hard to see what is best for the child when there are so many competing feelings.

To the judges of the Family Court, I wish for you to have the divine gift of discernment which was given to King Solomon because the Government of the day has presented you with a very sharp two-edged sword. One edge will allow you to cut a meaningful future for children by giving them a better relationship with their parents, through the gift of a shared life. With the other edge, you have the power to divide the life asunder and potentially inflict psychological wounds upon the child. Unfortunately, the law exceeds the current body of research, and we are all embarking on a journey into untested limits of the mental health world.

In conclusion, as parent or decision-maker, there is no such thing as neutral behaviour. Everything will have an impact on the future of that child. We already know separation is not a short-term crisis, but a long-term developmental change for the life of the child. There are no simple solutions, and the professional research is incomplete. My hope and prayer is that parents will be more willing to seek help in addressing their relationship problems and spare their children from the problems arising from separation. However, if separation and divorce are unavoidable my hope is for parents to find ways to put aside their emotional difficulties and differences and truly share the life of the child rather than dividing the child in half. Shared care or divided life? The power is in your hands.

Key Points

- From the child's perspective, what is best for them is for the parents to fix the relationship. If it can be properly fixed the children need the parents to stay together. If that is not possible, parents still need to fix the relationship sufficiently to parent co-operatively.

- Children not only need "shared care" but "best care". There is no single living arrangement applicable to all families and circumstances. The key aspect is for children to have a meaningful long-term relationship with both their mother and father, structured to balance everyone's needs.

- The choices are sharing the life, dividing the life, or not being involved in the life. Only shared care is going to truly benefit the child.
- Shared care or divided life for the children? The power is in your hands.

Index

A
access arrangements *see* custody and visitation
Ackerman plan, meaning 217
age of children, impact on parental contact 76, 208–14, 247
alienation of children from a parent 86–90
anger *see* emotional issues and separation
attachments between children and adults 54–8, 71, 208
distinguished from bonding 57

B
blaming behaviours 105–6
bonding 54, 208
distinguished from attachments 57

C
caretaker position, meaning 36
children
coping mechanisms 70–8
decision-making processes 66
development of 51–70
emotional security 51–3, 74–6
involvement in court proceedings 174–8
psychological impact of separation 7–9, 29, 84, 209, 256, 260

sexual behaviour 118
children's rights 109–12
co-parenting model 133–4, 140
collaborative law *see* mediation
communication between parents 112–115
communication book 113
conflict in relationships
    effect on children 42
    impact on visitation arrangements 224
    see also violence in relationships
consistency in parenting styles 142–3
contact arrangements *see* custody and visitation
controlling parents 137–8
counselling 35, 155–6
    conflict situations 117, 203
    for depression 39
    legal requirement for 30
court proceedings 165–8, 170–2, 201
    disadvantages 187
    involvement of children in 174–8
    reaching agreement 161
    stress in relation to 163
courts, role in the legal system 163–4
crossover parenting model 139–40
custody and visitation 202, 215–17, 228–9
    impact of children's age 90, 208–14, 218, 247
    impact of parents' circumstances 204–6

    no-contact arrangements 238–42
    stepchildren 247
    see also shared care

D

depression 37–9
    impact on children 38–9, 100–1
discipline styles 140
dispute resolution 161
divided care 258–9
    distinguished from shared care 14
divorce
    effect on children 28–9
    history of in Australia 23–5
domestic violence *see* violence in relationships

E

emotional development of children 60–2
emotional issues and separation 33–42, 105–7
    anger in children 62–3
    overburdening children 100–3
employment *see* separation; shared care
ex-partners, creating a positive image of 151–2

F

Family Court *see* court proceedings
family home *see* parents, proximity to co-parent
Family Law Amendment (Shared Parental Responsibility) Act 2006 (Cwlth) 11

see also shared care
fantasy images of parents 90, 239–40
financial issues *see* separation

G
grief *see* emotional issues and separation
guardianship of children *see* custody and visitation
guilt *see* emotional issues and separation

H
honesty *see* truth

I
isolation of children from a parent 9

J
judges, role of 170–2

L
lawyers
role of 165, 168, 174
selection of 172–4
legal system 166–7
living arrangements *see* custody and visitation
loyalty demands on children 104–7

M
mediation 160–1, 170, 183, 185–8
money *see* separation, financial implications

N
nesting, meaning 227–9
new partners, impact on children 152–3, 228

no-contact arrangements 238–42

O
over-protectiveness, effect on children 61
overburdening children *see* emotional issues and separation
overnight contact 75–6, 102–3, 208–14

P
parallel parenting model 134–5, 138, 140
parental alienation syndrome, meaning 86–7
parenting plans *see* custody and visitation
parenting styles 133–40, 142, 223
parents
impact of behaviour on children 15, 16, 41, 42, 83–109, 142–3, 151–2
impact of new partners on children 152–3
proximity to co-parent 154–5, 204–5, 222
reaching agreement 159–68
property settlement *see* separation, financial implications
proximity of parents *see* parents, proximity to co-parent
psychological assistance *see* counselling

R
refuse 9, 71, 115, 230, 248
reject 9, 21, 195, 251
relationship life cycle 161–2

remote control parenting model 136–9
rights of the child *see* children's rights
role models 89

S

safeguarding children from harm 238–42
secure base behaviours, meaning 51–2
separation
  alternatives to 28, 257
  emotional impact 33–42
  employment implications 45
  financial implications 32, 43–4
  impact on parental contact with children 18–19, 199, 202
  process of 33–4
  psychological impact on children 7, 29, 84, 209, 256, 260
  see also divorce
separation of siblings 247
serial monogamy, meaning 26
sexual abuse 46–7, 49, 117, 119–20
shared care 217–25, 257
  custody and visitation models 217–21
  distinguished from divided care 14
  employment implications 32, 221–2
  legal basis 11
  meaning 11, 15
  practical considerations 204–5, 222
  psychological basis 134
  social impact 12–14, 30, 32
siblings
  effect on visitation arrangements 213
  separation of 246–8
sleeping arrangements *see* overnight contact
stepchildren, contact arrangements 247
stress 163
substance abuse 242–5

T

taking sides *see* loyalty demands on children
therapy *see* counselling
truth 93–5

V

village 68, 254, 255
violence in relationships 46, 49, 117, 120–1
effect on children 28, 95–6, 122, 238–9
no-contact arrangements 238–42
visitation *see* custody and visitation
visitation arrangements, impact of substance abuse 243–4

W

Wallerstein, Judith, research findings 67–9

About the Author

Dr Phil Watts is a well-known Western Australian clinical and forensic psychologist and is a past president of the WA branch of the Australian Psychological Society forensic college. After completing a master's degree in clinical psychology in 1989, he worked for the Department of Community Development and Ministry of Justice before commencing a private practice in 1994. He has 30 years' experience in private practice. Currently, he is the director of Mindstate Psychology which is a mixed practice involving forensic assessment and clinical treatment of families, adults and children.

A significant aspect of his practice includes running training programmes for various professionals. Of particular note are his training seminars for lawyers and national training to health professionals on how to give evidence in court, report writing for court and assessment of risk in clinical practice.

Dr Phil presents at national and international conferences and workshops. He is the author of six books including, *How to Find Love and Not a Psycho* (2020).

With over 2200 appointments as Single Court Expert in the Family Court he has witnessed first-hand the terrible impact of separation upon the lives of children. The book *Shared Care or Divided Lives* is written to help families avoid going to court or, if they are already in the legal system, provides helpful understanding of some of the ways to buffer children from the conflict.

Additional copies of *Shared Care or Divided Lives*, to find out about Dr Phil's other titles, or to make contact with the author:

Ogilvie Publishing/Mindstate Psychology

PO Box 393

South Perth, 6153

Western Australia

Phone: 61 8 9450 1618

Email: info@mindstatepsychology.com.au

Website: Www.mindstatepsychology.com.au

www.ingramcontent.com/pod-product-compliance
Lightning Source LLC
Chambersburg PA
CBHW070537010526
44118CB00012B/1159